Pragmatic. Relevant. Engaging. *The Complete EdTech Coach* folds in authentic experiences with the voices of those involved. This authors interweave the realities of where educational technology has been and where instructional technology is going. This is a book full of reflective questions to ensure that all learners are kept at the forefront.

—**Kristina V. Mattis**, EdD

In *The Complete EdTech Coach*, Adam Juarez and Katherine Goyette provide a strong model for effective coaching in education. Examples provided throughout the book give the reader a better understanding of what organic coaching looks like and why it's more effective than just providing professional development or trainings, especially with tech-resistant teachers. The focus is not on pushing the latest edtech in classrooms but on students and how to support their teachers in providing the best activities for learning, whatever form that may take. The authors share both their failures and successes, giving guidance for how this work can be done with teachers and students as the driving force instead of a top-down approach. I recommend this book to current coaches, those who inspire to be coaches, and even campus technology teacher-leaders.

—**Dianne Csoto**, teacher

The Complete EdTech Coach is a book that builds a bridge between technology in education and the human beings who use it. Katherine and Adam share their philosophy about the tools and strategies they apply throughout their edtech coaching experience. This book helps you reflect on how to respect and honor others' learning journeys, a pivotal component to build an organic edtech coaching experience.

—**Perla Zamora**, edtech coach

Adam and Katherine's passion for student success and learning are apparent throughout this book. The on-the-job experiences they bring in will be authentic and meaningful for any edtech coach. I love their organic approach and focus on the learning and the 4Cs of education to target teacher and student success. If you are an edtech coach, I would highly recommend this book.

—**Kim Mattina**, technology teacher, host of *The Suite Talk*,
GCT, GCE, GfE Gold Product Expert

The Complete EdTech Coach is what edtech coaching could be and should be: practical ideas with purposeful implementation. This book focuses on the education aspect of edtech, i.e., how a coach or tech TOSA can best facilitate the teacher-tech relationship so that it is mutually beneficial for teacher and student. *The Complete EdTech Coach* focuses on the learning first and then the tools that best help learning manifest itself in engaging and authentic ways. It helps us understand that an effective edtech coach should be "in the know" and "on the go." *The Complete EdTech Coach* puts people before programs and teachers before technology. This is a book for new or seasoned edtech coaches / tech TOSAs, educators, and administrators looking to best support colleagues and staff in facilitating deeper learning and wider connections while wielding the power and possibilities of tech.

—**Vanessa Heller**, middle school educator,
Inquiry/PBL trainer, and site tech innovator

Adam and Kat (AdaKat) bring a human and real side to edtech coaching. For years AdaKat have let their creativity, accessibility, and passion shine as they inspired both local and global teachers. They have shared their passions in presentations and on social media, and when I heard they were putting their ideas into a book, I was beyond excited. In *The Complete EdTech Coach,* you will learn how to power up your coaching with tips on badging, certifications, and building your PLN. This book will not only help edtech coaches empower teachers; it will also empower students and student's voices. I recommend this book for both new and seasoned edtech coaches who really want to take their coaching to the next level.

—**Ben Cogswell**, kindergarten teacher

If you are an edtech coach, want to be one, or know someone who is one, this book is a must-have. With their many years of experience in the edtech coaching world, Adam and Katherine give many pointers on how to tackle this difficult but rewarding job. I guarantee that this will quickly become the #1 go-to resource for novice and experienced edtech coaches alike. Thank you, Adam and Katherine, for sharing your expertise and knowledge!

—**Sylvia Duckworth**, author of *Sketchnotes for Educators* and *How to Sketchnote*

This book is great! I love the personal anecdotes and how Adam and Kat are open and honest about their journeys in edtech coaching. They really give a guide that takes people from wherever their current starting point is and moves them along to become a great coach. I also appreciate how Adam and Kat acknowledge and endorse using a PLN. They really make it about being better together and growing in our profession.

—**Kim Calderon**, high school teacher

There are many books about teaching, but far fewer about teaching teachers. Katherine and Adam have spent nearly half a decade perfecting techniques alongside teachers and getting real results— and that's what makes *The Complete EdTech Coach* different. Katherine and Adam share techniques and methodologies that have teachers asking for more rather than asking how soon the training will be over. For coaches who want to excel, implement tech at a high level, AND make teachers happy, this book is just the right thing at just the right time!

—**Jon Corippo**, CUE teacher emeritus, former assistant superintendent, and coauthor of *The EduProtocol Field Guide* and *The EduProtocol Field GuideBook 2*

Technology is everywhere today, and, in many ways, it is easier to use than ever. Technology should not only be about making our world easier but ultimately, making it better. I appreciate the way Katherine and Adam provide meaningful strategies for those who support our classrooms and those who, in turn, help our students use technology to empower themselves now and in the future. If you support teachers using technology in the classroom, this is a great read.

—**George Couros**, author of *The Innovator's Mindset*

Adam Juarez and Katherine Goyette do not disappoint. They bring their knowledge, wisdom, and experience to the masses with their first book. *The Complete EdTech Coach* brings their guiding foundations and principles of educational technology together, and it's a testament that technology is just a tool—not always the answer—and sound pedagogical practices and learning must come first.

—Tim Costello, teacher

The Complete EdTech Coach is an essential read for any educator looking to scale the heights of technology integration in the post-COVID, twenty-first-century learning landscape. Adam and Kat operate as your own personal edtech guides to help you explore the sometimes scary digital unknown by sharing their own personal experiences, asking the essential questions, and leading with learning to bring you into deeper and more relevant connections in core content areas. Be prepared to take your instruction (and coaching) game to the next level!

—Michael Abramczyk, STEM lab facilitator

If you have any interest in working with people and tech, this book is for you. I've known and followed Adam and Kat for several years, entirely through an online PLN relationship, but I know them well. I was even part of their wedding as a virtual bridesmaid. So I know that Adam and Kat speak from experience and the heart, and with this book, you're getting real and relevant experiences.

—Stephanie Filardo, teacher

Adam and Kat prove that edtech coaches are the bridges that provide support for a new, enchanting teaching philosophy and style. This book lays the groundwork for edtech coaches everywhere to build and support their districts, sites, and teachers with compassion and understanding. This book is phenomenal and will change the way edtech support is given.

—Rosalinda Jaimes, teacher and cofounder of TechFairies

I can't wait to dig into this book further. It is filled with practical applications and real stories of *organic* edtech coaching in action! When we lead with learning we see far better results for student and teacher success. This is a must-read for all educators!

—**Jen Francone**, administrator of educational resource services at TCOE

Adam and Kat infuse their readers with their love of technology integration. In *The Complete EdTech Coach*, they give edtech coaches a practical game plan for their work in their school, their district, and beyond. Organic edtech coaching will help coaches grow their faculty's skills, build their own skills, and reap the rewards of job satisfaction.

—**Tom Mullaney**, Google Product Expert

Teachers need the support of coaches, not just professional development. Teachers and students are the important "who" in classes. Ultimately this book will help you move beyond the "why" and support the "who."

—**Crystal Miller**, principal

Finally, a guide to help those helping teachers! *The Complete EdTech Coach* is all about coaching from the heart, collaboratively and with empathy, and valuing the educator where they are.

—**Katie McNamara**, teacher librarian

If you support the use of technology in the educational system, this book is a must-read. *The Complete EdTech Coach* is the perfect resource to help educators use technology in meaningful and practical ways with their students.

—**Tara Martin**, educator, author, public speaker, and director of public relations and communication, Dave Burgess Consulting, Inc.

THE COMPLETE EDTECH COACH

THE
COMPLETE EDTECH
COACH

AN ORGANIC APPROACH TO
SUPPORTING DIGITAL LEARNING

ADAM JUAREZ AND KATHERINE GOYETTE

The Complete EdTech Coach: An Organic Approach to Supporting Digital Learning

© 2020 Adam Juarez and Katherine Goyette

This book is available at special discounts when purchased in quantity for educational purposes or for use as premiums, promotions, or fundraisers. For inquiries and details, contact the publisher at books@daveburgessconsulting.com.

Published by Dave Burgess Consulting, Inc.
San Diego, CA
DaveBurgessConsulting.com

Library of Congress Control Number: 2020944793
Paperback ISBN: 978-1-951600-56-3
Ebook ISBN: 978-1-951600-57-0

Cover and interior design by Liz Schreiter
Editing and production by Reading List Editorial: readinglisteditorial.com

This book is dedicated to the memory of Adam's father, Lou Juarez. Lou coached Adam in various sports and exposed him to some legendary coaching figures. Lou was always a massive supporter of Adam's coaching both in the classroom and on the athletic field.

Contents

INTRODUCTION

WHY EDTECH COACHES?

Devices are being deployed in schools across the globe. Many administrators have never been students or teachers with this many student devices in the hands of the learners they serve. Teachers are being called upon to alter the way they teach to include student use of technology. This comes at a time when teachers indicate they are overwhelmed with standardized assessments, initiatives, and the ever-changing landscape of education. Recently, the global pandemic caused by COVID-19 has altered the education field in a manner unforeseen. Educators and administrators alike pivoted toward distance learning. Distance learning roadblocks include school closures, internet connectivity issues, the lack of availability of student devices at home, educator unfamiliarity with tech tools, and edtech companies providing an overwhelming amount of options.

Students are evolving as well. Teachers across the world report that students today are more easily distracted and have more difficulty focusing for extended periods of time than was the case in previous generations. Platforms such as Netflix, Snapchat, TikTok, and Fortnite can contribute to this attitude. Students are accustomed to receiving on-demand, instant gratification. Cyberbullying, inappropriate online content, and predators also lurk within this connected digital world.

During the fifteenth century, the printing press brought knowledge to a vast number of individuals. Similarly, the digital accessibility tools in our midst today can allow more and more learners to build knowledge in the way that works best for them. Our learners can accomplish much more than we realize, provided they have the tools. As educators work to increase access to content for students, particularly our students with special needs, we guide them toward the best strategies to continue learning outside of the classroom. As the digital divide starts to narrow, technology serves to promote equity as students can access content with their peers, whether face-to-face or virtually. Examples include speech to text, translation tools, and other accessibility features. Students become resourceful. They learn to utilize technology to increase their accessibility to knowledge in the world.

This all unites to create a real necessity for edtech coaches. Teacher education and Beginning Teacher Induction programs, in our experience, have not yet prepared teachers to meet the demands of the modern, connected digital world. Administrators and veteran teachers, too, have little to no experience dealing with these new issues, let alone leveraging the skills today's generation possess. Too often, the issues this generation deals with, along with the unique skill set they possess, are scoffed at. ("These kids today . . .")

What if the most embarrassing and perhaps inappropriate moment of your adolescence had been posted on a public platform for all to see, creating a digital tattoo that could never be completely erased? The challenges this generation faces are real. It is our job as educators to increase our understanding of the realities of our current students' world, in order to prepare them not only for the future, but for the reality of today. An edtech coach leads teachers in promoting digital citizenship within the context of their content and curriculum. Edtech coaches can coach classroom teachers to use digital platforms such as Google Classroom and Flipgrid to provide safe environments for students to practice positive digital citizenship.

For much of the early twentieth century, you needed an operator to communicate across long distances. Whether by telegraph or telephone, you relied on this person to connect you. For educators today, edtech coaches are the "operators" connecting them to the most meaningful edtech integration.

IF YOU KNOW EDUCATORS WHO ARE WORRIED ABOUT STUDENTS IN THIS DIGITAL AGE, WE, THE EDTECH COACHES, HAVE THEIR BACK.

Educators often don't have the time to learn the newest, most effective ways to deal with these issues. Technology innovates quickly. Teachers struggle to keep up. An edtech coach, dedicated to keeping abreast of iterations in the industry, saves precious time by supporting and guiding educators through the constant evolutions. Educators *need* edtech coaches.

We had the pleasure of attending a lunch and learn session with Jimmy Casas at ACSA (Association of California School Administrators) Conference in 2018. In his session and book, Jimmy explicitly states that he does not have any answers, only experiences. We love the message encompassed within that statement.

LIKE ANYTHING IN EDUCATION, THERE IS NO MAGIC BULLET.

We also have shared experiences and our own action-research that provides support to other edtech coaches. These stories help us know that, as edtech coaches, we are not alone in this.

We are not the only educators searching for the best way to serve those in our midst. Jimmy's session is geared toward administrators, and he frequently talks about how the challenges they encounter were not taught in "principal school." This is even more the case with edtech coaching. One can get a degree in educational administration, but there is no degree for supporting teachers, districts, and administrators through edtech coaching.

Like many edtech coaches, we both were thrown into the fire with no experience. We were told, "Hey, you're good at tech. Go teach the staff how it's done." Talk about easier said than done! A quick internet search reveals that the research platform Crunchbase determined that there are over thirteen hundred EdTech platforms in the US alone, all vying for preeminence. It is one thing for a person to know how to use a single tool. It is quite another to be able to teach someone else how to leverage a tool in a classroom (after convincing them of why it is important in the first place). And it's a full-time job to keep teachers updated with the newest platforms, the outdated ones, and the platforms that are updating to provide accessibility, ELL, SEL, and other support.

Edtech coaching is uncharted territory. When we began as edtech coaches, there was no playbook to guide us. We were encouraged to write this book to share the lessons we have learned on our journey. Our approach to edtech coaching is based on our experiences, and the philosophies and techniques we recommend grew organically based on the needs of those we serve. We have learned from our failures and successes. Our goal has been to write the edtech coaching book that we wished had been available when we ourselves began.

And please remember that our approach is organic! This means we encourage you to build your personal edtech coaching playbook, using this as a springboard for your own style of teaching. We do not offer a one-size-fits-all approach. Rather, we share our learnings to prompt reflection, provide ideas from the field, and encourage you to continue the great work you are doing.

FOR WHOM IS THIS BOOK WRITTEN?

The goal of this book is to guide edtech coaches toward leveling up the great work they are already doing, using the expanding network of tools at their disposal. We present an organic approach that validates your professional autonomy as an educator and empowers you to leverage technology to transform learning for students. There is no one-size-fits-all approach. As an edtech coach, part of the job is to honor the experience of the educators we serve while simultaneously helping them continue to grow their coaching toolbox.

> ORGANIC COACHING DOES NOT ASK YOU TO DITCH WHAT WORKS OR TO START FROM SCRATCH. RATHER, ORGANIC EDTECH COACHING BUILDS UPON YOUR STRENGTHS AS AN EDUCATOR.

Whether you are new to edtech coaching, looking for guidance regarding the ins and outs of the job, or are a seasoned edtech coach looking for a fresh approach, you are our focus. However, this process (like so much in education) relies on departments working together. (And as a note to instructional coaches: this book will provide you with effective methods of technology integration plus tips for effective coaching in and out of classrooms.)

Early in our edtech coaching careers, we were under the impression that we would coach teachers by training them in all the innovative apps and strategies learned through our PLN (personal learning network) and at conferences. We would train them via slide decks and sit-and-get PD (professional development). Edtech coaching in this manner is not organic. This style of coaching and integration is not natural. In fact, it is not coaching at all—it is better referred to as training. There is something very unnatural about learning an edtech app or strategy out of the context of your classroom and learning goals.

Coaches, How Can You Benefit from an Organic EdTech Coaching Model?

Organic edtech coaching starts by first observing teachers and identifying their academic learning goals, in their own natural environments. It does not begin with technology apps. Again, we don't lead with the tech, we lead with learning. Organic edtech coaching suggests apps and strategies only after the teacher and coach have identified learning goals and strategies that enhance their particular learning environment. In this manner, the integration of edtech is natural and organic. The apps and strategies are embedded within the learning goals. The integration happens *during* the planning, not before or after. Edtech integration before or after planning makes the learning and the edtech seem like two separate things. Organic edtech integration weaves the tech in naturally for a best fit.

In this book, you as a coach will learn tips and strategies for maximizing your coaching in a way that personalizes the experience for those you serve. Whether you are an instructional-content coach looking for effective methods of embedding technology integration into your content-based coaching or an edtech coach seeking to increase your impact with teachers of various grade levels and/or content areas, the stories and resources in this book will build your capacity for connecting with those you serve for the benefit of students.

Administrators, How Can EdTech Coaching Bring Value to Your Role?

Are you an administrator looking to leverage the effectiveness of an edtech coach in your organization? We offer practical methods for working collaboratively with your edtech coach.

An edtech coach can help administrators transform staff meetings, PLCs (professional learning community), and other forms of professional development. In our experience as edtech coaches, we have had the opportunity to help administrators power up their staff meetings and PD. These meetings formerly consisted of administrators passing out various handouts and paper exit tickets. Meetings and PD were often sit-and-get where PowerPoint slides were essentially read word for word to a room full of educators. When leaders ask educators to increase student engagement in the classroom but run meetings that do not provide active learning opportunities for teachers, it sends a mixed message.

ADAM

Early in my coaching days, I had the opportunity to work with my administrators to reflect on the goals, structure, flow, and interactivity of meetings and PD. I recommended Google Classroom as a platform for conducting meetings and PD. As these leaders became more proficient, we brought in a variety of other apps and strategies. Immediately, the administrators saw how Google Classroom helped save time distributing materials and how much less paper was used. Agendas, minutes, and slides were posted in Google Classroom. This improved teachers' ability to see the presentation and better engage. No longer did they have to squint to see the projector screen. Teachers could better follow along and access necessary materials from their own device right in front of them. Don't assume teachers are less present with a device in front of them. The device can create an opportunity for them to be more present than ever.

Google Classroom allowed the administrators to link to other apps such as Quizlet, Google Forms, and Flipgrid to make the meeting more interactive. At the same time, teachers were beginning to be inspired to try these apps seeing the administrators use them. Google Classroom also provided a back channel for teachers to ask informal questions without disrupting the flow of the meeting or PD.

By turning to an edtech coach, these administrators were able to power up their meetings and PD in ways they likely would never have considered. Coaching the administrators to integrate edtech is also a great way to have teachers view the administrator as a model. If the administrator models integration for all to see, it carries more weight when they and the edtech coach suggest it.

Teachers, How Can EdTech Coaching Impact Your Practice?

What can you expect from an edtech coach? An organic edtech coach provides opportunities to collaborate and seeks to understand the strengths of the teachers they serve. They look to build upon those strengths and align with individual teaching styles and passions.

Katherine had an experience speaking with a group of educators who indicated they were facing challenges in utilizing technology in a meaningful way with their students. In hearing the concerns and asking a series of questions, it was clear that in order to ensure that coaching met their needs, it would be helpful to observe them in their natural environment . . . the classroom. There is no one-size-fits-all approach, so it is important to validate the great work the teachers were already doing and build upon their strengths.

KATHERINE

I asked if the teachers would feel comfortable with me observing their instructional environment to better guide our collaborative work toward impactful technology integration. The educators agreed, and I was welcomed into their rooms. I quickly noticed a trend. In each classroom, technology was used with an all-or-nothing approach. When students used devices, they had no paper, physical books, math manipulatives, or dry-erase boards on their desks. Students did not speak with classmates. Often, students had headphones on, furthering their isolation from each other. And anytime a student had a low-tech or no-tech tool with them, there was no digital device to be found. The problem was not that these educators were afraid of technology, or that they did not believe it could be a powerful tool. Rather, they had not yet found ways to seamlessly integrate technology into the solid instructional strategies they had been using before the devices had been available. This is where teachers can benefit from an edtech coach. I introduced these teachers to the 4Cs lesson design (which you will see later in this book) and we collaborated together to design experiences for students that led with learning, not with tech.

An edtech coach is a supportive guide, encouraging you and providing ideas that fit within the context of your classroom and instructional style.

- PART I -

PHILOSOPHY

"WE NEED EDTECH COACHES IN SCHOOL TO HELP MAKE TECHNOLOGY MORE ENGAGING AND AVAILABLE TO STUDENTS AND TEACHERS IN THE CLASSROOMS. TECHNOLOGY CAN BE SCARY BUT AN EDTECH COACH CAN MAKE THE USE OF TECH IN THE CLASSROOM A SMOOTH AND EASY TRANSITION FOR ALL TEACHERS."

—JESSICA REED, MA,
SPED TEACHER FROM ALABAMA

– CHAPTER 1 –

WHAT IS ORGANIC EDTECH COACHING?

"Edtech coaching has been invaluable in my teaching and classroom structure. Being in the thick of things in my lesson building, I might not see opportunities for technology to be used, especially in a lesson I have been doing for years. Katherine has given me a plethora of ideas and resources that are easy to use and my students are very engaged in."

—Krystal Poloka, Science and STEM Teacher,
Woodlake Valley Middle School, Woodlake, California

We use the term *edtech* (educational technology) rather than *tech* (technology) purposefully. First and foremost, we are educators. An edtech coach is not IT (instructional technology). Our job is not to fix printer settings or to order new light bulbs for projectors. YouTube videos can teach you how to use a technology tool. An organic edtech coach focuses on building and guiding: building relationships with educators of all levels, and guiding them in designing learning experiences that accelerate student growth toward academic goals. An important component of an edtech coach's role is to be a connected educator. Being a connected educator includes growing their

PLN in addition to staying abreast of trends in edtech via the various certifications offered by edtech companies. These certifications include such accolades as Google for Education Certified Innovator, Microsoft Innovative Expert, and Newsela Certified Educator just to name a few.

Districts that employ tech coaches rather than edtech coaches are wasting their money. They may as well send their teachers to YouTube or hire additional IT staff. Edtech coaches are credentialed teachers. As mentioned above, administrators should be guided to leverage your experience as a classroom teacher and not diminish your value by using you as a tech tool trainer. Effective edtech coaches do not focus on tools. Rather, they guide educators to lead with learning, to weave technology into lessons in a way that facilitates student collaboration, communication, creativity, and critical thinking.

When edtech coaches lead with learning rather than tech, they may find that there are instances during which it is more effective to use a no-tech or low-tech strategy to best meet the learning goal.

KATHERINE

I met with a teacher recently who was interested in using Google Forms to collect data for her students. As I asked this teacher deeper questions about the learning goals of the lesson, it became clear that in this instance, the technology would be a deterrent, a distraction, and time waster for the task. I listened for a moment and then said, "To be honest, I think Post-its on a few pieces of chart paper would be most appropriate for this task." The teacher paused. "Interesting," she said. "So, I don't have to use technology all the time . . ."

ADAM

Since I connected with Sylvia Duckworth, who has written several books about sketchnoting, I firmly jumped on the sketchnoting bandwagon. Sylvia is an expert on it and will show you many ways to sketchnote with and without tech. As I have promoted sketchnoting with the teachers I serve, I used a paper-pencil sketchnoting model. No tech at all. Teachers I coach one-on-one and work with in PD sessions realize afterward that no tech was used, and it is OK. Then they ask about how tech fits in. I tell them, in this case, it comes afterward. Sketchnoting fulfills the learning while tech, whether it be via website design, a collaborative video platform or screencasting, enhances the learning demonstrated by the paper-pencil sketchnoting. The learning is enhanced in how the sketchnoting gives kids a visual method of expressing ideas while the tech offers a platform to display their learning to an authentic audience for feedback. Edtech in this manner is organically integrated.

As an edtech coach, never forget that you are a teacher first. Our focus must always be on learning first and technology second. Do not be afraid to suggest low-tech or no-tech options if they are most conducive to the task. This will increase rather than decrease teachers' respect for you as a coach who has their best interest in mind. This shows teachers that you are not there for your own agenda of increasing tech implementation, and reveals your vision of putting student learning at the forefront—no matter what. Edtech coaches who guide teachers to no-tech solutions when most appropriate for the learning goal are far more likely to be heard when they suggest a technology tool.

WHEN TECHNOLOGY INTEGRATION IS ORGANIC, IT EMERGES NATURALLY. IT IS NOT FORCED.

Organic edtech coaching occurs in a teacher's, administrator's, or fellow coach's natural edu-environment. Organic edtech coaching believes that coaching trumps professional development. It requires boots-on-the-ground coaches who are in classrooms, PLCs, planning meetings, staff meetings, and PD (professional development) sessions. Facilitating PD centered on an app or strategy in the staff room is not organic integration. Organic edtech coaches are on the front lines helping those they serve to integrate edtech while coaching them to identify and plan learning goals and targets. Organic edtech coaching leads with learning, never with tech.

Organic edtech coaching is inclusive of all educators. Educator and author Michael Fullan suggests you "use the group to move the group." You may want to start with your more eager-to-learn educators to build a buzz and some confidence, but do not shy away from those who are hesitant. The biggest coaching wins you can have are with those who are initially hesitant. Organic edtech coaching builds upon and validates the strengths of all educators, especially veterans who may be uncomfortable with edtech. Teachers may fear you are trying to change how they teach, but as educator and edtech coach Joe Marquez says, "Edtech doesn't change how you teach, but how you reach students."

Organic edtech coaching does not begin with a technology-centered framework. Rather, it is learner centric. Edtech integration is best cultivated through the lens of the 4Cs (collaboration, creativity, communication, critical thinking). The 4Cs focus on the learners we serve, not simply the technology they use. In our experience, if you plan with the 4Cs in mind, the tech will take care of itself.

– CHAPTER 2 –

COACHING TRUMPS PD

I t is through job-embedded coaching that we build educator belief in students' abilities, provide just-in-time support, and foster relationships. Be with those you serve. Begin by walking among them, present on the physical or virtual campus, and then join them in their work with students.

As a walking coach, be explicit about your intent, and don't be the sheriff. In most situations, edtech coaches are teachers on special assignment (TOSA). In the hierarchy of a school district, they are lateral or at the same level as teachers. In many instances, edtech coaches, and other content coaches, too, are viewed as quasi admin. If this is the case, teachers may view the edtech coach as a sheriff of sorts, which can make coaching relationships difficult. Being viewed as the evaluator is common.

NO PD CAN REPLACE THE POWER OF AN EDTECH COACH'S PRESENCE IN A TEACHER'S CLASSROOM.

In the very beginning of Adam's edtech coaching career, he nearly fell into this trap. He was inadvertently asked to be a sheriff. At this time, the district schools were moving toward being one-to-one in the classrooms. The schools had Chromebook carts (COWs) teachers could check out. His first edtech coach mandate was to get teachers trained on Gmail and the rest of G Suite. At this time, training the teachers to implement the usage of Chromebooks was in its infancy. After a district admin walk-through, the superintendent was curious as to why the vast majority of the Chromebook carts were sitting idle in the storage room and not being checked out and used. The superintendent reminded the site admin team that they paid good money for these Chromebooks and they have an edtech coach. They wanted to see their investment in technology put to good use.

Receiving constructive criticism from your boss, in any form, can be uncomfortable, so it seemed natural to work with the site admin team to game-plan getting those COWs out of the pasture. In an effort to act on the feedback of the superintendent, Adam was instructed to report to admin which teachers were using the Chromebooks and how they were being used. This is a perfect example of a situation where an edtech coach is being branded as a sheriff. To avoid this trap, Adam responded, politely, that following this path could make him lose all credibility and trust with teachers. Again, this wasn't the site admin's intent, but it was an easy trap in which to fall.

But there was an alternate solution—one that would better support and sustain an organic edtech coaching model. If the admin team was provided with a menu of apps and strategies in which teachers and students had been coached after classroom visits, they could then walk classrooms and have conversations with teachers about the 4Cs and implementation. This approach did not portray the edtech coach as a sheriff: it supported the superintendent's vision for implementing edtech, gave the site admin team a frame of reference, and maintained credibility and trust with teachers.

In Katherine's first year out of the classroom, she spent a great deal of time and thought creating a digital walkthrough form that she completed when walking classrooms. While this was designed with positive intent, it was far too complex and felt evaluative to the teachers that were being served. The form had checkboxes that were selected when particular instructional strategies and technology were integrated in the classroom. It quickly became apparent that, as edtech coaches, it is important to provoke reflection among the teachers we serve, not to appear evaluative. While Katherine communicated to teachers that the walkthrough forms were simply documenting a snapshot of time, they felt evaluative nonetheless. There were so many checkboxes on the form that even if great things were happening in the classroom, teachers focused on the boxes that were not checked. It felt negative.

The next year, Katherine reworked the feedback form. The content of the form came from the staff themselves, not from her. The forms asked what the teachers would like Katherine to look for in the classroom visits. Their response? "Keep it simple." These teachers asked that the revised form contain only four checkboxes, reflecting the presence of students engaging in the 4Cs. Katherine also added a short answer option to note "Commendations." Any inquiries or suggestions were done in person, not in writing on an impersonal form.

The simplified form was very effective. Educators loved both the simplicity and the fact that the content came from their vision for improvement. Katherine took a summary of the form to a staff meeting one day. In the past, an edtech coach would have presented the results and provided suggestions on how to improve. However, this would feel evaluative and top-down. Instead, Katherine gave results to the educators themselves, who celebrated growth and made their own plans as to how to continue to improve their methods of using no-tech, low-tech, and high-tech methods to engage students in the 4Cs. The approach was organic. It grew according to the needs and observations of those doing the work.

EDUCATORS LOVED BOTH THE SIMPLICITY AND THE FACT THAT THE CONTENT CAME FROM THEIR VISION FOR IMPROVEMENT.

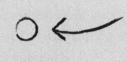

Building relationships is crucial. Katherine recalls walking through a classroom and witnessing a teacher panic as her students were unable to join her Google Classroom. Neither the teacher nor the students could find the classroom join code on a page they'd used only a day prior. As an edtech coach, Katherine knew there had been an update of the Google Classroom platform and was able to provide immediate support to this teacher and her students. If an edtech coach had not been present on campus, this teacher may have abandoned this valuable organization and communication platform out of frustration. Furthermore, Katherine was able to provide job-embedded, personalized support. Organic edtech coaching provides on-the-spot support during the implementation process. PD alone is not enough. As we coach using an organic method, we build relationships and connect with those we serve during instructional planning, classroom application, and reflection.

We like to say, "Coaching trumps professional development." What is the difference, you ask? Professional development often consists of a talking head disseminating information for an hour or two via sit-and-get instruction. Many times, this type of professional development does not include follow-up by the presenter with a coach, in a teacher's classroom. Coaching, on the other hand, provides not only demos and seminars, but boots-on-the-ground follow-up in classrooms. Coaches are in teachers' classrooms providing feedback based on what they are teaching in the moment. The feedback comes in many forms. It may be a Post-it left on a teacher's desk, an e-mail generated by a digital form completed via the coach's tablet, phone, or laptop, or even a conversation during prep or lunch later that day. The feedback loop must move quickly or momentum will be lost. It is often said that feedback is most effective when it is specific, timely, and actionable. Otherwise, it falls flat. Organic edtech coaches walk among those they serve to ensure feedback as such is possible. This is an organic, context-based approach. Edtech coaches are in PLCs and planning meetings providing feedback and offering tips. Coaching provides individualized support, not blanket tips. The tips given to an ELA teacher may look completely different than those given to a mathematics, history, or science teacher.

Adam's experience as a soccer coach was helpful. He couldn't give the same support and advice to every one of his players. The skill and experience levels varied too greatly. There were teams with players who had a wealth of experience, skill, and previous elite coaching. At the same time, these teams also had players who had never put on a pair of cleats or stepped foot on a competitive soccer field. The experienced elite players were often given more challenging, nitpicky feedback along with advice on how to coexist with lesser-skilled, inexperienced players. In contrast, these lesser-skilled, inexperienced players were given feedback regarding topics such as the basics of the game, how to properly pass the ball with their instep, or how to head the ball with the forehead instead of closing their eyes and letting the ball hit the top of their head.

Organic edtech coaches who work with teachers follow the same pattern. The edtech integration coaching we provide to a thirty-year teaching veteran who still owns a flip phone and shuts off their e-mail on weekends and vacations is much different than the support provided to the third year Nearpod PioNear who has accounts on Instagram, Snapchat, Facebook, and other social media platforms.

Edtech coaching is cross-curricular. It is learning objective and 4Cs centric. It is not content specific. If academic content is the "what," technology is part of the "how." Edtech coaches personalize the professional learning experience with teachers by varying the technology-integration methods, the how, to meet different content areas and experience levels.

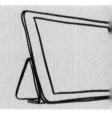

AS AN EDTECH COACH, BE SURE YOU REMAIN TRUE TO YOUR TITLE. YOU ARE A COACH, NOT A PD DELIVERY SYSTEM.

Anyone can learn to use tech tools and create a training session slide deck through the magic of YouTube and/or a Google search. Coaches build relationships. They get to know their people. They are among those that they serve, always on the lookout for the best ways to customize support to meet the individual needs of each educator with whom they work. As an edtech coach, you are in a people business. It is all about relationships. You can personalize the learning experience *only* when you've taken the time to get to know those you serve. Be in classrooms, whether physical or virtual, engage in conversations, and observe.

We have facilitated countless hours of PD sessions for educators. While these sessions can be valuable in training teachers to use tech tools effectively, when done alone they often fail to result in considerable change in classrooms. Consider the following research, "When professional development merely describes a skill to teachers, only 10 percent can transfer it to their practice; however, when teachers are *coached* through the awkward phase of implementation, 95 percent can transfer the skill."[1] This is even more the case with technology. Consider the example of the teacher who could not find the Google Classroom join class button she'd easily accessed only a day prior. The technology moved more quickly than the time it would have taken to develop, schedule, and deliver additional PD. Even better, administrators love in-class coaching because subs are not required! PD often requires administrators to hire subs in order for teachers to leave the classroom to engage in a workshop. Coaching, on the other hand, does not require the teacher to be out of the classroom. This is effective *and* fiscally responsible.

We have had the opportunity to teach intern teachers (those who are in the process of taking classes to obtain their teaching credential, but are already working in classrooms as full-time teachers). In a class titled Learning to Teach in the Twenty-First Century we spend many hours with these intern teachers, guiding them in tasks that will empower them to integrate technology in meaningful ways. It's a powerful opportunity to teach them about pedagogy, leading with learning, and the 4Cs. We also engage these teachers in using many technology apps and strategies as students, to give them as real an experience as possible. This hands-on approach supports them in the implementation process once they apply these tools and strategies in their own classrooms.

---

1   Jessica Cefalo Osich, "Mathematics instruction in Pre-Service Undergraduate Programs in the State of Maine" (Doctoral thesis, University of New England, 2018), 33, https://dune.une.edu/cgi/viewcontent.cgi?article=1176&context=theses.

Brianne was a student in the aforementioned class that Katherine taught for teacher interns. Katherine also visited Brianne's school site, separate from the intern class, to provide job-embedded in-class coaching. Brianne once remarked that she learned more in thirty minutes the first time Katherine was in her classroom than she had learned in hours engaging in activities as a student in the teacher-intern program. Brianne had loved the teacher-intern class and would come back each week with stories of what tools and strategies she had tried. But the job-embedded coaching had proved much more valuable. Here is Brianne's perspective:

"In my experience through a teacher-intern program, the classes designed to teach teachers how to manage their classrooms in the twenty-first century, can be, by nature, a bit two-dimensional. You have no students or real-life scenarios to contend with, only a theoretical 'perfect class' in your mind. On-site tech training is much more beneficial in that aspect because you're trying out suggestions in real time to see if it works in your classroom. You learn quickly what works and what doesn't for your students, and the class benefits from the experience. I have also found benefits in this type of training because it forces you to try things out of your comfort zone. Instead of slowly sticking your toe in the waters of technology, you're cannonballing into the deep end with a helpful lifeguard there to rescue you in case of drowning. I'm thankful I've taken some risks in trying new things and my students are thankful as well."

—Brianne Underwood, English Language Arts Teacher, Woodlake Valley Middle School, Woodlake Unified School District

Brianne's testimony reinforces our experience. Coaching trumps professional development. Organic, job-embedded coaching occurs when we walk and observe. It supports both students and teachers. Teachers build confidence, and they are willing to move forward in the implementation process because a coach is right there beside them during the process.

– CHAPTER 3 –

PD: WHERE IMPLEMENTATION GOES TO DIE

In the professional development sessions we facilitate, we consciously spark conversations with educators, ask questions, and do all we can to customize the session to meet the needs of those in the room. The energy in the room is apparent as educators actively engage in tasks that leverage tools and strategies they can apply to their classrooms.

After these professional development sessions, however, momentum slows to a near halt during the implementation phase. Administrators have told us they have stopped sending teachers to conferences because there is no large impact on classrooms upon their return and very little change for students. These teachers come back to their school sites full of ideas and excitement, but somehow this does not translate to classroom implementation.

What causes the gap between professional development and action? How can we affect work in classrooms?

Coaching can bridge the gap between PD and implementation. As a teacher, it is one thing to learn tips and tricks in a professional learning session full of other teachers. It is quite another thing to learn how to implement these tools alone, in the context of your own classroom. This is where personalized coaching comes in. As an organic edtech coach, it is vital that you support teachers by coaching them during the planning, classroom implementation, and reflection phases of teaching.

ADAM

The first time I learned of the magic of Flipgrid, a collaborative video platform, one of my first thoughts was how well this would work with our Spanish teachers. Flipgrid allows students to respond to teachers' prompts with video rather than merely via text. Much like the message board in an online college course, students respond to the prompt and can also respond to classmates using video. On two separate occasions, I met first with a veteran Spanish teacher and then with an intern Spanish teacher. Coaching them up, I began by asking each to focus on his/her/their learning target and standard. After the discussion on the academic content, I recommended using Flipgrid to help kids verbalize and showcase their Spanish speaking. Utilizing this platform would give the teacher a great insight on student ability. I did not lead with Flipgrid. I led with the teachers' learning goals, their individual contexts. From there, we planned and incorporated Flipgrid into their lessons. Their lessons and learning targets were completely different. I facilitated a demo for one period and had them take the reins during the remainder of their class periods. We debriefed afterward. From that point forward, these teachers have used Flipgrid regularly as a method of formative assessment and student engagement.

Had Adam merely given a whole staff PD on how to start with Flipgrid, these two teachers might not have been successful with it. They may not have seen how the tool could align with their particular academic content goals, with their groups of students. They may have given up during the classroom implementation process. Both teachers, self-admittedly, are not tech savvy. Knowing this, Flipgrid integration had to be born of one-on-one coaching, organically.

Over the past few years, we have been collecting feedback via conversations and surveys from the educators and administrators with whom we work. Many leaders and teachers are initially hesitant to invite us into classrooms to work with teachers and students. Educators do not want to be judged. Leaders want to maximize training hours. As an edtech coach, we should slowly shift our work to include more classroom coaching and less PD via thoughtful conversations during coaching sessions, stories of success thanks to leaders who trusted me to use this approach at other schools, and testimonials from others. Teachers are learning that our role is to support, not to condemn. We focus on enhancing the great work educators are doing, not on rating them on a framework. Leaders notice that teachers apply and sustain more learning from our time in their classrooms for thirty to forty minutes at a time, than they do from hours in a PD session. A principal recently remarked, "I know that my teachers are implementing their learning from your classroom coaching by asking the kids. The students tell me. And the coaching is working."

One of the schools Adam serves, Orosi High School, was honored to host the 2019 edition of Tech Rodeo, our county's annual EdTech conference. As the host, we had many of our district teachers attend. It is no coincidence that after the conference, Adam was inundated with requests for further help with the amazing PD they received. This being said, PD is not enough. Follow-up is crucial for teachers to successfully implement.

If you send a teacher to a conference and they don't have any future support or follow-up, implementation of what they learned will be extremely difficult and highly unlikely. This may result in burnout and disillusionment by the teacher. At Tech Rodeo, a large number of teachers learned the awesomeness of Pear Deck, a platform for making digital presentations interactive for participants. The Monday following the event, teachers reached out for training, tips, and information about whether or not they should pursue a premium license. Since then, Adam has met with these teachers individually, assisted in their implementation of Pear Deck, and helped them obtain premium licenses.

At that same event, Adam's friend Joe Marquez gave a presentation about Google's "secret menu" with tips and tricks regarding Google, of which most people are unaware. A good number of Adam's teachers attended this session. Similar to the experience with Pear Deck, the

Monday morning after the conference his in-box was full of requests for follow-up and help with what these teachers learned from Joe's session. Long story short, PD is not fully effective without the follow-up and support of proper coaching.

KATHERINE

As organizer of the aforementioned Tech Rodeo, I often wonder if the experience creates a lasting impact with educators. Coincidentally, I was at a school site on a day when a couple of teachers spoke to the school staff about their experience attending the event. As the teachers spoke, I was encouraged by their ability to share their learning with other teachers. They relayed information about specific apps they had begun implementing in their classrooms to fuel academic learning. This being said, the teachers that spoke have classrooms of their own. They are not edtech coaches. They do not have time contracted to be outside their classroom to work with their colleagues to implement this new learning. These teachers shared their learnings from Tech Rodeo with staff. And their colleagues were interested, but it is only because of the time I had allocated to be in their classrooms after the conference that we were able to move this excitement and interest into implementation. It is important to build capacity from within, to spark change organically through the influence of teachers sharing with their colleagues. An edtech coach builds upon this via job-embedded, in-class support.

The teachers in the examples noted above had a wonderful experience at an EdTech conference. They left the day grateful for the learning, eager to implement new strategies and tools in their classrooms. But PD, even engaging, interactive, applicable PD, often fails to result in the implementation we hope. This is because job-embedded coaching is vital to the process. Musicians spend countless hours of their lives learning, practicing, and performing in orchestras, concert bands, and jazz ensembles. Musicians can learn new skills in a private music lesson and then practice their part of a piece until it is perfect. After hours of practicing on their own, muscle memory takes over and the musician can play their part without thinking. The same is true with the other musicians onstage during a performance. However, this doesn't exclude the need for rehearsals and coaching during performances. Just as the conductor of an orchestra listens and provides job-embedded guidance during whole-group rehearsals, teachers benefit from a coach who observes and supports the implementation of new learning into a classroom environment. Knowing how to use a tool perfectly does not necessarily translate to effective use once an educator steps into a classroom of students with varying needs, personalities, and skill levels.

> IF YOU SEND A TEACHER TO A CONFERENCE AND THEY DON'T HAVE ANY FUTURE SUPPORT OR FOLLOW-UP, IMPLEMENTATION OF WHAT THEY LEARNED WILL BE EXTREMELY DIFFICULT AND HIGHLY UNLIKELY.

Katherine's first teaching experience was at a private music school, where she worked with groups of piano students ages infant through adult. When she was preparing her first group of students for their recital, Katherine made the mistake of forgetting about the gap between learning and implementation. She'd worked hard to prepare the students with the skills needed and the practice time on their individual parts for their ensemble pieces. But they did not spend the necessary time to prepare together, as a class ensemble. Students were not able to take individual learning experiences and easily apply their parts to a group context. In other words, it's not possible to expect a seamless transition to implementation. Similarly, we must coach teachers through the process of applying strategies they have learned in the context of their classroom.

Elite soccer players have mastered countless skills, tricks, and moves. Those things do not equate success on the field without a coach to guide them in the tactical awareness of how and when to unleash their skill set. As a teenager, soccer superstar Cristiano Ronaldo was known to be a bit of a show-off. In matches, he spent much time exhibiting his deft touches, fancy stepovers, and blinding speed. Under the tutelage of legendary Manchester United coach Sir Alex Ferguson, Cristiano evolved from a trickster who didn't provide many goals to an unstoppable goal-scoring, trophy-winning machine. Even if teachers have mastered an app, it remains beneficial to coach them through classroom implementation process. Mastery of a tool is not sufficient for effective pedagogical implementation with students.

– CHAPTER 4 –

MEASURING YOUR IMPACT: BEYOND NUMBERS

Traditionally, when we think of data, we think test scores, charts, and tables that you can analyze in a spreadsheet. Meaningful tech integration isn't measured that way. Measurement comes not from numbers on a spreadsheet, but from observation of the 4Cs (collaboration, creativity, communication, critical thinking) in the classroom, followed by a review of student artifacts. The focus is evidence of student learning, which includes the deliverables students produce to demonstrate this learning. Remember, in academic-content classes, tech is not the "what," it is part of the "how." Teachers lead with the "what," their academic learning goals. Edtech coaches guide teachers in using technology toward a new "how" that meets the needs of today's students, to engage them in the 4Cs.

It is from active student engagement in the 4Cs that we can gauge student learning and plan accordingly. Edtech coaching is not something that can be measured properly and completely by looking at standardized test scores. Furthermore, edtech coaching does not fit well within a traditional coaching cycle. Traditional coaching cycles seek to analyze the results of pre- and post-assessments within a content area. Within a content area, this is effective, but it does not work for organic tech integration. Putting tech integration into a traditional coaching cycle model flips the focus toward the tech itself. It inadvertently sends the message to teachers that they are to lead with tech and not with learning. And it makes tech seem like yet another thing on their plate. With this in mind, tech integration must be measured with the 4Cs and action-research, not with checklists of the tech being used. Tech is the "how," evidence of which is seen by student engagement in the 4Cs. It is best measured through observation. This observation of what students produce is our action-research. This occurs when teachers are coached to ditch the "sage on the stage" teaching model and adopt a "guide on the side" model.

Action-research is not always quantitative. It is more than numbers. For edtech coaches, the data is seen as expanded teacher toolboxes. It is seen when the teachers you have coached grow their PLN as a result of your coaching, to further their learning.

Edtech coaches are successful when:

- Teachers and students alike respond to your coaching by implementing strategies between the times you visit.
- Educators independently seek additional coaching. The more often teachers request to level up their learning, to build upon the strategies you have introduced them to by adding to their toolbox, the more you know their work is making a difference in the classroom.
- Students brag about the work they have done as a result of your coaching. This is edtech coaching action-research data.

It's a great idea to spend time before the school day, during lunch, and after school in staff lounges. We position ourselves where staff members congregate, to build relationships, to increase our visibility, to offer support. We have discovered that this practice has also allowed us to collect evidence of implementation. Time and time again, educators see us in the lounge and share reports of how they have been implementing strategies used in prior classroom coaching sessions. As these teachers share their excitement, other educators hear their success stories. This leads to conversations and questions about how they, too, might try the strategy in their classrooms. Educators who may have been hesitant to integrate technology into their classroom now see coach-to-teacher collaboration in action among their peers. And this can cause them to feel more comfortable seeking support from either the edtech coach, or from educators with whom they work. In intentionally placing ourselves in locations where we know educators will be, conversations organically occur. And this also gives us feedback on how our edtech coaching has impacted students. This helps us measure our impact.

If you want to reach teachers, if you are looking to show teachers that technology has the power to transform their teaching, leverage their desire to make an impact with students. In-class coaching allows an edtech coach to respond to the sigh of, "I'm just not good with technology." It shifts the focus from the teacher to the student. This is the research we are looking for, impact with students. Student engagement with the 4Cs, and the teacher's excitement about this new "how" to teach content reveals that coaching was effective. Testimonials like these affirm the work of an edtech coach and help us see the fruits of our labor. But they also help us fight for our jobs, illustrating the value of our coaching to the administrators who decide whether or not to keep our positions. And positive results begin to spread with other teachers.

As an edtech coach, your end goal should be to positively impact students, to result in classroom environments that empower learners to utilize technology to access, curate, and create content. The best method of reaching students is often through educators. But we must never forget the ultimate goal is to serve students. And we can often reach educators through students. It is our job to help teachers place technology into the students' hands to enhance their learning.

Edtech coaches are stretched thin. We often serve multiple grade levels, sometimes multiple sites, and in some cases, multiple districts across a relatively large geographic area. This is where students can become scaffolds for teachers. When students are empowered in this way, both the students and the teachers themselves benefit from increased learning. Because we are unable to be at each site, in each classroom, as an on-call support as often as we'd like, we have built the capacity of students to support their peers, and even their teachers, as you will see in more detail in Katherine's example of an edtech coaching vehicle in Part III of the book.

AS AN EDTECH COACH, YOUR END GOAL SHOULD BE TO POSITIVELY IMPACT STUDENTS, TO RESULT IN CLASSROOM ENVIRONMENTS THAT EMPOWER LEARNERS TO UTILIZE TECHNOLOGY TO ACCESS, CURATE, AND CREATE CONTENT.

Peer support is essential. The most impactful part of our coaching role is the time we spend in classrooms with students, building their capacity to provide support to each other when their teacher is unsure how to proceed in the future. Again and again, teachers tell us that it is the students themselves that teach them tips for efficient technology use. We have seen teachers encourage students to create screencast tutorials that will be used in their class for the next year's class of learners. This empowers learners as it shifts responsibility of teaching from the teacher to the students. And it is action-research that provides evidence of the effectiveness of our coaching.

Katherine began working with teachers at a school site where she was told she would encounter resistance. The educators had already expressed their many concerns to administration regarding the decision to provide each of their young students with a Chromebook. Not only did the teachers feel nervous using a Chromebook, they also believed the young learners they served would not be able to handle it as well. Initially, Katherine spent a few hours with each teacher team, building their capacity in managing and using these student devices in their classrooms. The teachers requested additional one-on-one time to learn and plan. They did not feel confident rolling out the devices to students until they were more comfortable themselves. While the hesitation remained, Katherine gently insisted that the next coaching session would be in their classrooms. Time would be spent not in the teachers' lounge planning, but in their classroom environment—with students.

KATHERINE

The day I arrived, the Chromebook carts had not been opened. These teachers did not yet have the confidence to open the Chromebook carts in my absence. I was neither surprised nor disappointed. I remained positive and supportive. "No problem, that's why I'm here," I said. "This is a process and by the end of today you will be further along than you were yesterday." I would love to be able to say that my time in these classrooms immediately changed the teachers' perspectives. It would be an amazing story if by the next month the students were using the Chromebooks to research, engage in digital academic conversations, and practice listening/speaking skills using the power of video. But this is a true story, meant to inspire leaders to continue coaching when progress seems slow, to continue supporting each and every teacher, and to never stop believing in the power of relationships, patience, persistence, and time. We call upon teachers to never give up on a student, but do we have the same mentality with the teachers who challenge us? We must remember that learning is a process, mindset shifts take time, and we are all in different places on our learning journeys.

In Katherine's second year working with these teachers, she had a few hours with each of them approximately seven times during the year. Since their initial planning meeting, 100 percent of that time was in classrooms with students. The progress the students made by the beginning of that second year was astonishing. They accessed e-books on their Chromebooks and created recordings of themselves reading the text aloud. They utilized Google Keep's drawing feature to document their growing understanding of number sense. They produced typed narratives. The aforementioned activities occurred even when Katherine was not on-site to provide support. What gave the teachers the confidence to open the Chromebook carts for students when she was not present? How did they become comfortable engaging students in these activities?

The teacher told Katherine, "Oh, I still don't know what I'm doing." The teacher chuckled and continued, "But I don't have to remember everything, the kids help each other. There are enough students in my class that remember what you showed them, that I don't have to have all the answers." This is the power of including students in your work with teachers. It is the students themselves that can build the capacity of not only their peers, but also of the educators who serve them. Edtech coaches maximize their impact by not only giving educators permission to learn from their students, but encouraging them to do so. A pedagogically solid edtech coach empowers educators by empowering students.

Organic edtech coaching will not occur if a coach sits in his or her office most of the day preparing slide decks in prep for voluntary after-school PD for educators. Effective edtech coaching does not consist of sit-and-get PD workshops on district-mandated PD days. Organic edtech coaching requires a vehicle created by the coach, not something prepackaged. To be organic, it must be born out of the needs of the teachers and students being served within the context of the unique climate and culture of the school.

But what is an edtech coaching vehicle? How do we build one?

ADAM

My edtech coaching vehicle (Google Certified Innovator Project), Cardinal Innovation Center, is a physical and virtual space created to facilitate coaching. The space allows me to curate student work created via coaching. At the same time, it is a growing, living learning resource for teachers and students alike. An edtech coaching vehicle will help you produce evidence when asked about your impact. Your reply is based on the foundation of your vehicle. The vehicle showcases evidence of the students utilizing technology to communicate, collaborate, think critically, and demonstrate activity as a result of content-based learning experienced as a result of coaching with educators.

A PEDAGOGICALLY SOLID EDTECH COACH EMPOWERS EDUCATORS BY EMPOWERING STUDENTS.

Your edtech coaching vehicle showcases the work of your students, teachers, and yourself to a wider audience. Why a wider audience? The answer relates to the reasons many people dress up for church, weddings, quinceañeras, and other special occasions. When we know others are looking, we tend to try harder. As part of the Cardinal Innovation Center website, Adam will tweet out links to student work constantly. The looks on the kids' faces when they learn that their work received likes and comments from teachers across the world—the look of empowerment—is priceless. When educators learn that other teachers from across the globe are inspired by their students' work, they feel inspired and empowered to continue integrating tech and are more open to continued coaching. Whatever your assignment is, no matter the community you serve, create a vehicle for edtech coaching. Your job may depend on it. Your vehicle provides tangible evidence that the work you do is valuable, needed, and essential.

– CHAPTER 5 –

START WITH WHO

More times than we can count, we have heard administrators and teachers alike refer to the need to "start with why." While it is more effective to start with "why" than to start with "what" or "how," the "start with why" phrase puts the focus on vision (often a vision handed down from an individual or a committee). Rather than starting with "why," we always start with "who."

We are here for students and educators.

We are in the business of serving others.

As an edtech coach, do not focus on your vision, your district mission statement, or your leaders' "why." While all of these may be compelling to the individual(s) who wrote them, they divert focus away from the most important part of the equation . . . the "who." "Who" should always be on the forefront of our minds. Our "who" should drive us.

KATHERINE

In my first year out of the classroom, I believed I had a compelling "why." I had seen the power of technology in my own classroom. It enabled students to create rather than merely consume content using multiple media methods. Halfway through the year, my students were granted one-to-one iPads through a pilot program. Student writing improved as I instituted a daily, standards-based writing prompt using a learning management system through which learners constructed responses, viewed peers' writing, and then learned to give each other timely, descriptive feedback based on a rubric. Students accessed the internet and conducted research to bolster their arguments for a class debate; they searched for YouTube videos that demonstrated their learning of pathos, logos, and ethos; they synthesized their understanding of content in various forms of digital note-taking. I vowed to do all in my power to provide digital opportunities like these to as many students as I was able. I felt it was my moral imperative to promote equitable student access to technology to anyone that would listen.

Katherine quickly learned that the educators she was working with did not necessarily believe in her "why." That vision did not resonate with these educators. Technology felt like one more thing on their already full plate of duties. These educators had their own passions, their own "why." An edtech coach can preach "why" until they are blue in the face, but that does not equate to sustainable change for these educators.

As coaches, we must learn that it is *not* all about us. We do *not* have all the answers. What worked for each of us as a teacher is not a magic bullet. Educators are individuals, with their own passions and strengths. If we are to make an impact with these teachers, we must personalize our approach, we must start with the "who," the educators we serve and the students in their care. Our approach must be organic, to grow based on environment. It was only after Katherine began to ditch her own agenda and build relationships with those she served that she was able to provide personalized support that aligned with the needs and contexts of their classrooms and students. And that was when meaningful change began—change that impacted learners.

The world is increasingly aware of our need to stop teaching Wi-Fi students with landline strategies. This idea embodies the philosophy of starting with the "who." Education and edtech coaching needs to focus on the "who," the human children we serve. What are their needs? What are their interests? And most important, what unique life experiences and skills do they bring to the classroom? The current generation does not know the world without the internet. As Jon Corippo and many others say, "teach as if Google exists."

Starting with the "who" lends itself to organic edtech integration. It is a natural fit. Recognizing the limitations of teaching only land-line strategies to a Wi-Fi generation speaks to this. Most educators can recall the world and education without the internet. The current generation of students does not. This fact can be your first step into organic tech integration.

Knowing our "who," the current generation's experience of being immersed in technology since birth, helps set the foundation for coaching teachers on why edtech integration matters. Often, teachers will resist by indicating that coaches are pushing technology on them because we ourselves happen to be good at it. We are techie. We enjoy gadgets and new strategies. It's our thing as edtech coaches. Counter this resistance with the "who"—the current generation's experiences, learning needs, and expectations. The fastest way to a teacher's heart is through their students. They can tell the coaches *no* all day, but it's usually more difficult for them to tell the students *no*.

KATHERINE

Consider the following quote from a teacher I coached in her class-room with students, "My students were highly engaged in using Google Classroom, Screencastify, and Google Keep. Every time I announced that Ms. Goyette was coming, the students roared with excitement and made it a point not to miss school that day. They counted down the days until she was coming because they were eager to learn something new." Her excitement is about her "who," the students she serves.

Students today are seemingly obsessed with Snapchat. What better way to help students identify themes, claims, and more than incorporating BookSnaps, invented by educator/author/speaker Tara Martin. BookSnaps combines reading strategies with features of Snapchat. In a nutshell, BookSnaps is a strategy that can greatly increase engagement and comprehension with reading. It is versatile and can be employed to digitally mark text, cite textual evidence, identify claim, and more. It leverages students' love of images by adding stickers, emojis, filters, and other images to text. This engages students in academic content using a platform with which they are familiar and enjoy. To build upon this strategy, BookSnaps can be used to further student proficiency using a variety of other tech tools, thus fostering further skill building. Since Snapchat and mobile devices may be blocked and/or restricted at a school, BookSnaps can be created using non-Snapchat tools such as PowerPoint, Google Slides, and Seesaw.

BookSnaps are just one of many strategies that help connect learning to students' lives. Strategies such as BookSnaps prove the need for an edtech coach. With so much being asked of teachers these days, edtech coaches have their eyes and ears open for these clever, cutting-edge, innovative ideas to help the teachers and students they serve. Edtech coaches build bridges between cutting-edge, innovative pedagogy to the teachers they serve. They connect the tech-laden lives of today's students with content and curriculum.

"Academic conversations" has been a popular phrase in education for the past few years. Yes, students need the ability to converse about content using academic language and vocabulary, and engage in discussions while citing evidence. Yes, it is also true that students today often prefer to communicate via forms of text rather than speak out loud to a live human person. Adults often worry that students' digital devices have negatively affected their abilities to relate to others.

To address this issue, let's start with the "who." Students today have digital communication skills that can easily be leveraged as first steps toward full-blown academic conversations. As educators, we must know our students. Rather than throwing students into the deep end and expecting them to start talking, we leverage *their* skills. We build on *their* strengths.

Begin with posting prompts in digital platforms such as Google Classroom or Google Groups to have students respond to the prompt and each other virtually via digital text. Digital communication skills are vital for success in higher education courses done online. Once students are comfortable responding to each other via digital text, teachers can guide them in verbalizing their thoughts via Flipgrid or screencasting. Once comfortability with virtual, electronic forms of discussion have been fostered, then live in-person academic conversations will be much easier for today's students. When we start with the "who," leveraging students' tech skills and savvy, we can scaffold them toward academic conversations. This is much more effective than prompting them to simply start talking. Starting with the "who" makes the learning and edtech integration organic and more sustainable. Edtech coaches can bridge our students to the educators we serve. Our role is vital for the sake of connection.

HIGHLIGHT REEL: PART I

TAKEAWAYS

- Technology serves to promote equity, and edtech coaches are essential to bridge the gap between teaching and access to technology.
- Edtech coaches are teachers first.
- Administrators and teachers are searching among thousands of platforms for effective methods of embedding technology. Edtech coaches cut through the clutter.
- When technology integration is organic, it emerges naturally. It is not forced.
- Coaching can bridge the gap between PD and implementation.
- Edtech coaching vehicles showcase the work of your students, teachers, and yourself to a wider audience.
- Always start with "who."

QUESTIONS FOR REFLECTION

- Why is edtech coaching a vital part of your organization?
- How might you communicate the value of an edtech coach with stakeholders?
- In what ways have you personalized learning for those you serve? How might you use an organic approach to improve the way you connect with your learners?

BRAINSTORMING GUIDE

List some ways you can show that you're a teacher first:

List some ways you can avoid being the "sheriff":

Quickly list edtech vehicles you admire and some reasons why:

Describe a challenge you've encountered in your work with an administrator or a teacher:

How did you handle it?

How could you improve communication with those you serve?

PART II

PEDAGOGY

"EVEN THOUGH I RECEIVED CHROMEBOOKS AT THE TAIL END OF LAST YEAR, I DID NOT KNOW HOW MUCH POTENTIAL THERE WAS IN USING THEM. I WAS SURPRISED AT HOW CAPABLE MY STUDENTS WERE AT ADAPTING TO USING TECHNOLOGY IN LANGUAGE ARTS AND MATH. I LOOKED AT IMPORTANT CONCEPTS STUDENTS WERE EXPECTED TO KNOW AND MS. GOYETTE HELPED ME LAUNCH THESE IDEAS USING TECHNOLOGY. SHE SPENT QUALITY TIME BEYOND WHAT WAS SCHEDULED TO HELP ME PUT THEORY INTO PRACTICE."

—LUPE GOMEZ, FIRST-GRADE TEACHER, WILSON ELEMENTARY, DINUBA UNIFIED SCHOOL DISTRICT

– CHAPTER 6 –

LEAD WITH LEARNING, NEVER WITH TECH

Lupe's focus is not on the technology itself. Nowhere in her statement does she talk about the programs used. Lupe's students have used their Chromebooks to engage with various G Suite tools, quizzing platforms, and screencasting. But that is not what was most memorable to her. Her focus is on the students' connection to language arts and math, while utilizing the technology as a tool. The focus is on the learning, not on the tech. In planning with Lupe, many times after school and via e-mails in order to maximize the impact of the coaching sessions in the classroom with her students, we focused on the learning concepts first, and then used technology to enhance the learning.

Getting the teachers you serve to understand the organic concept of leading with learning, never with tech, is easier said than done. Adam's first, truly organic edtech integration success occurred with a middle school ELA/history PLC. He was invited to join the PLC for some planning days. During these planning discussions, the teachers led the conversation. As they identified learning goals, targets, and standards, Adam strategically interjected ways in which technology could be used to help them meet these goals, targets, and standards.

His suggestions came while they planned, not after the planning had been completed. Embedding it in the process of planning itself makes it organic. Had suggestions been provided *after* teachers had finished designing their lessons, the integration of edtech would not have been as natural. Any suggestion would have served more as an autopsy and could have created frustration. What teacher wants to return to the planning process after they believed it had already been completed?

That middle school ELA/history PLC continues to be fertile ground for organic edtech integration. The team consistently reaches out to Adam for support and he still takes part in their planning days. Organic edtech integration led to a sustainable model of coaching. As new members have joined the team, they have quickly jumped on board with edtech integration. The reason the relationship with this team is ongoing and sustainable is because Adam did not lead with his technology agenda. Teachers led with their own learning goals. They owned the planning process and, consequently, they sought ways to use edtech to meet student learning goals.

OUR JOB AS EDTECH COACHES IS NOT TO MERELY TRAIN TEACHERS ON HOW TO USE TECH TOOLS. ORGANIC EDTECH COACHING IS ABOUT LEARNING, FIRST AND FOREMOST.

It may be difficult to message your role as an educator first and technology coach second. Even for edtech coaches, the learning is sometimes best facilitated with a no-tech or low-tech tool. Educators, particularly at the elementary level, often post a daily schedule on the board for their students to see. For each assigned time, an academic content area or task is often listed (mathematics, reading, writing, science, social studies, physical education, art).

Note that "technology" should not be listed next to a time frame. Educational technology is not a content area in and of itself: it is a means of accelerating learning of academic goals. Rather than planning something like "students will learn to create presentations using

Google Slides or PowerPoint" during "technology time," we must flip the verbiage and the focus. Educators need to be focused on academics first and tech second. Consider a goal such as "students demonstrate understanding of figurative language in a text by creating a multimedia presentation." This is leading with learning, not with tech.

As an edtech coach, you may get pushback from administrators when you suggest no-tech solutions for teachers' learning goals from time to time. If this is the case for you, consider the following. Google is arguably one of, it not the, most innovative, influential technology company in the world. And yet, Post-its cover the walls, ideation and collaboration occur on dry-erase tables and walls, and communication often occurs IRL (in real life) when people are present with each other. Google places a large emphasis on in-person team building. The company engages in collaboration via virtual means as needed, but we have seen low-tech and no-tech methods of engaging in communication, collaboration, creativity, and critical thinking in each Google office we have had the privilege to visit, tour, and work in.

Technology use, by itself, does not prepare students for the world of today. We have been to countless classrooms in which students stare at their devices, engaged in a program that adjusts to their academic needs using learning analytics. Students have headphones on and are engaged not with peers or a teacher, but with the device itself. Sometimes administrators indicate that this student use of technology by itself is a magic bullet. They argue that the method is high on the SAMR ladder (a framework designed to support teachers in using technology in the classroom), and that it is an example of a personalized, automated experience for students at a redefinition level. The argument is that this learning opportunity could not be accomplished without technology.

TECHNOLOGY USE, BY ITSELF, DOES NOT PREPARE STUDENTS FOR THE WORLD OF TODAY.

Districts spend a great deal of financial resources on adaptive learning programs, which promise to raise student achievement with time on task on a computing device. Many districts mandate that students engage with the program a minimum number of minutes per week, and they track time to ensure compliance. While these programs are purchased and implemented with positive intentions, this use of technology can seem to imply that an automated program, artificial intelligence based on an algorithm, is more effective than learning from human beings—than teachers and peers. While artificial intelligence could not occur without technology, it does not replace the power of relationships with individuals—particularly in an environment of distance learning. Connections are key. Relationships trump tech every time.

When mandated to use an adaptive learning program, some teachers appreciate the break in their schedules they get when students engage on a computing device, alone, void of communication, collaboration, or creativity. As students spend time with their eyes glued to a screen, educators sometimes spend that time catching up on grading student work.

We are often told that research shows that students must have a minimum number of minutes engaged in these programs in order to meet a particular growth goal. Educator Casey Agena remarks, "We throw around the words *efficacy* and *fidelity* a lot in terms of [adaptive technology] platforms, but we need to really ask the question on the impact on students." Administrators may monitor minutes on a platform, but how often do they collect evidence of student learning? Is technology truly more effective than a teacher, simply because of the minutes staring at a screen?

By evidence, we do not mean quantitative data. Student learning can't be reduced to a number, to an amount of minutes. In our action-research, we collect evidence (via observations, student deliverables, etc.) that students actively engage in content by communicating, collaborating, thinking critically, and creating. We have not yet found a learning-adaptive software that fosters learning with a 4Cs lens. Edtech apps, programs, and the like are not magic bullets.

What is the right answer? If placing a device in front of a student is the most effective method of positively impacting learning, does it follow that teachers are not needed? And if this is the case, why have an edtech coach? All that would be needed is training in using the tool. The technology would become the teacher. Furthermore, with emerging concerns regarding screen time usage by students, and arguments that the digital age has created a generation of students who struggle to communicate on an interpersonal level, mandated minutes on a device may create problems.

Katherine had a conversation with a teacher who indicated that learning-analytic programs seem to be at a substitution level according to the SAMR framework. When we say substitution level of SAMR, we mean that a tech tool substitutes for an analog tool. For example, instead of using an actual, physical encyclopedia, use an online encyclopedia. The teacher remarked, "Learning-analytic programs are no different than the packets of work I disseminated to students, which I differentiated based on the skills in which they needed the most support." This was a perspective Katherine had not heard before. "Interesting," she said, "Though the programs use an algorithm to provide specific feedback to each student based on how they complete the work, in real time." The teacher smiled, "I was no different than the computer. I also gave feedback. I circulated the room and gave students feedback as they worked. But the difference was, I had a human connection with them."

It's a hugely important point.

Student learning cannot be put on cruise control. And no one learning-adaptive program, by itself, has a personal relationship with a student. Technology can never replace the power of a credentialed human being, a caring and competent adult, in the students' midst.

– CHAPTER 7 –

4Cs LESSON DESIGN

As edtech coaches who lead with learning, never with tech, it is our job to guide well-meaning administrators and educators toward the knowledge that there is a better way. Edtech coaches, with their understanding of edtech apps, strategies, and the 4Cs, are valuable assets to administrators on what apps and programs to explore, and how to implement and interpret evidence of student learning. We firmly believe in the power of educators to make a difference in the lives of students, via connection and relationships.

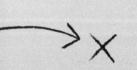

> EDTECH COACHING GUIDES EDUCATORS IN LEVERAGING TECHNOLOGY TO ENHANCE THE LEARNING EXPERIENCE IN A WAY THAT CONNECTS RATHER THAN ISOLATES.

We do not believe that technology itself can replace a teacher, nor do we believe that students learn best disconnected from a human being who cares for them. Organic edtech coaching rejects methods of technology use that disempower teachers and students.

Effective edtech coaches do not use tech for the sake of using tech. In order for technology to be integrated organically, we begin with those we serve. Just as Google places a large emphasis on in-person team building, organic edtech coaching starts with relationships, not with tech. The businesses of today are not looking for employees that can follow the directions on a screen. Rather, they are looking for problem solvers, communicators, creators, and collaborators.

ORGANIC EDTECH COACHING REJECTS METHODS OF TECHNOLOGY USE THAT DISEMPOWER TEACHERS AND STUDENTS.

Consider the results from the World Economic Forum regarding the skills that the companies of today (not the "future") are looking for in potential employees. Two of the 4Cs, critical thinking and creativity, are specifically listed. Collaboration is implied by the skills that include coordinating with others. Communication is a prerequisite for many of the skills listed, including negotiation and people management. In the next chapter we provide ideas for coaching teachers to integrate technology in ways that foster these skills.

Top Ten Skills in 2020

1. Complex problem solving
2. Critical thinking
3. Creativity
4. People management
5. Coordinating with others
6. Emotional intelligence
7. Judgment and decision making
8. Service orientation
9. Negotiation
10. Cognitive flexibility

It is vital that we not only prepare our students for college and/or careers but also that we provide equitable access to academic content in each classroom today. As educators, we design learning experiences to meet the needs of each and every student in our sphere of influence. When we focus on the 4Cs, we increase accessibility to meet the diversity in our classrooms. Universal Design for Learning (UDL), a research-based framework built upon a foundation of neuroscience, is designed to support educators in supporting each learner in their classroom. While the guidelines within the framework may be necessary for some students, they are beneficial for all. The 4Cs are embedded throughout the framework.

Examples of the 4Cs Infused within the UDL Framework

- Collaboration: guideline 8.3—foster collaboration and community.
- Critical thinking: guideline 3.2—highlight patterns, critical features, big ideas, and relationships.
- Creativity: guideline 7.1—optimize individual choice and autonomy.
- Communication: guideline 5.1—use multiple media for communication.

We have found that when we, as edtech coaches, focus on the 4Cs as the "how," students learn content and technology opportunities are organic and meet the unique and individual needs of the learners in our midst. And it works because it activates multiple networks within the brain.

KATHERINE

My son came home from school a few weeks ago and remarked, "Mom, I was in a block period class today for two hours. I left the class and realized I had not said a word." He indicated that students had used their school-issued devices to access content while their teacher spoke the majority of the class period. This teacher may have been struggling to get through content to meet a pacing guide and made the decision to disseminate information quickly. But that decision focuses on teaching and content. It neglects the most important part of the equation—student engagement with the 4Cs. We teach students, not content.

If content does not connect with the modern learner, we have lost. Educators may not be aware of the tools they can use to leverage students' strengths when applying technology to engage in the 4Cs. This is our job as edtech coaches. We provide and support the bridge between modern students and their teachers.

One way coaches can effectively help teachers connect with English learners is the 4Cs. In addition to being infused into the UDL framework, the 4Cs are also vital for ensuring that English learners have equal access to and engage with content. According to the 2018 California EL Roadmap, English learners require opportunities for peer assistance and small-group learning. Two of the 4Cs, communication and collaboration, can be specifically leveraged to provide these opportunities. In addition, the California EL Roadmap states that English learners require academic language support, which is buttressed with explicit opportunities for oral and written language skills development. When we foster the remaining two of the 4Cs, creativity and critical thinking, we allow additional opportunities to develop oral and written language skills.

As edtech coaches, we guide teachers in discovering ways to organically integrate the 4Cs via technology, when appropriate. In doing so, we ensure that opportunities are provided for all learners, including those with special needs and English learners. In our experience, planning with the 4Cs in mind leads to meaningful, natural, organic edtech integration.

As always, the tech is a means, not an end. When technology replaces student discourse with teachers and peers, when it prevents engagement in collaboration, communication, creativity, and critical thinking, well-meaning leaders sometimes blame the devices. This is clearly counterproductive to our cause of empowering students through technology use. The tech can facilitate student engagement with the 4Cs. And leading with the 4Cs ensures that technology is led by pedagogically sound learning. You will find that not only does a focus on the 4Cs resonate with teachers and administrators, it also prepares students to be leaders.

 AS ALWAYS, THE TECH IS A MEANS, NOT AN END.

– CHAPTER 8 –

PERSPECTIVE ON TECH FRAMEWORKS

Many educators and administrators begin with a tech framework, but in our experience, this approach is not organic. When we understand people's responses to change, we better understand why the 4Cs are a more effective way to measure edtech integration.

It's helpful for you as an edtech coach to understand the diffusion-of-innovation theory, made popular by Everett Rodgers. Coaching is an *inclusionary* sport. Understanding human response to innovation, to change, helps us more effectively personalize coaching to meet the needs of each teacher and administrator with whom we work.

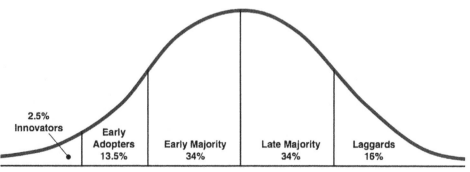

Source: Essential Marketing Models http://bit.ly/smartmodels

According to the diffusion-of-innovation model above, 2.5 percent of individuals will implement a new idea immediately. (And edtech is a new idea for teachers who have not yet integrated technology into their classroom.) Most educators are neither innovators nor completely unfamiliar to with educational technology. We tend to fall at various places on the diffusion-of-innovation model in different areas of our lives, even as educators. While a particular edtech coach may be considered an innovator in regard to emerging tech apps and tools, when seeking learning outside of the school setting, they may be hesitant in adopting other educational innovations, such as a new district initiative regarding academic interventions. Early adopters jump on board to a new initiative relatively quickly, perhaps after a single professional learning experience.

The early majority and late majority observe the early adopters. They may be interested in integrating technology but are hesitant to implement without the support of a coach, or suspicious as to the real benefit of a platform. The laggards are most hesitant to change.

When we reflect upon our experiences as educators and coaches, we see the diffusion-of-innovation theory in practice. Through our action-research, we have discovered the most effective methods that bring educators—from across the diffusion model—on board with edtech. It is possible to reach everyone, from the innovators to the laggards.

When Katherine was a classroom teacher, she was immediately drawn to an opportunity in the district to apply to be a pilot teacher for deploying iPads into the classroom for students' use. In this realm, the pilot teacher would be an innovator according to the diffusion-of-innovation model. Technology integration sparked a passion within Katherine that led her to conduct research, compile data, and speak with colleagues and administration to ensure that students would be granted this opportunity to transform their learning using technology. However, there were a limited number of iPads available districtwide.

The principal expressed surprise upon learning that Katherine's proposal for the program was to request one iPad for each of her thirty-seven students, as well as for two other classrooms. "You are asking for more than 10 percent of all available devices in the entire district," he remarked. Katherine pointed out that when a pilot program works, when the learning environment evolves and students are empowered to become more resourceful, creative, and collaborative, the message spreads and benefits even more students. By definition, such early innovator risk taking is not common with the majority of teachers. And that is OK. As coaches, we serve all teachers, not just the innovators.

AS COACHES, WE SERVE ALL TEACHERS, NOT JUST THE INNOVATORS.

Fortunately, the students were granted one-to-one iPads as requested. And at a meeting meant for the pilot teachers in the district, Katherine was introduced to the SAMR model. She was hooked by the idea of using technology for tasks that were previously inconceivable without it (redefinition). With every learning experience she designed for students, Katherine sought ways to reach the redefinition level of SAMR as often as possible.

Katherine was convinced that this model was an effective method for ensuring that technology in the classroom would transform the way we reach and teach our students. This became a driving goal, leading to Katherine leaving the classroom at the end of the year to take on a coaching position at a different school site, with teachers she did not know. She was eager to introduce the staff to her experience with SAMR.

The first day teachers reported back to work, the principal asked Katherine to speak at a staff meeting about goals for technology in the classroom. The principal recognized the success Katherine's classroom had experienced regarding technology integration and wanted to leverage this to inspire and lead colleagues toward more effective implementation of technology. Katherine had prepared some slides to present to the staff and was eager to speak about her experiences in transforming the way students had learned via accessing, curating, and creating academic content fueled by technology use.

During the presentation, Katherine shared screenshots of student work and showed images of specific ways students were using technology in the classroom for daily collaborative tasks. As a new edtech coach, she believed her message would inspire others to seek ways to replicate students' success. Katherine did not yet understand the diffusion-of-innovation model. Intentions were good, but as an edtech coach, she had not yet taken the time to determine the needs and passions of the staff.

As coaches, it is not about us. Effective coaching focuses on those we serve. These teachers did not want to hear other people's stories; they wanted to know how technology would fit into the context of their own classroom. The teachers listened politely, with limited interest, but it was clear this message was not resonating with them. This talk had started with the "what" rather than starting with the "who," the teachers sitting in front of her and their students.

The most ineffective slide in the entire presentation had the SAMR model displayed largely on the screen. As Katherine began speaking about how technology could be used to redefine the educational experience, the teachers became visibly anxious. The SAMR slide shifted the focus from students to teachers. It felt evaluative, and like yet another weighty educational initiative. And it placed a spotlight on the technology itself.

This was not a message of leading with learning first, followed by technology.

This experience was pivotal, showing the importance of ensuring that an edtech coach's message to teachers is simple and connects to concepts with which they are already familiar. Neuroscience reveals that the brain gravitates to the familiar, so new learning is strengthened and sustained when we make connections to context, to prior learning. SAMR felt foreign and overwhelming to these teachers. While they were an innovative staff in many ways (supporting English learners, supporting solid reading instruction that focused on people rather than programs, involving families and the community), teachers at this site covered various levels to the right of the innovator section of the diffusion-of-innovation bell curve in regards to educational technology. The moment these teachers saw SAMR, they were confused. On the next and final slide of the presentation, Katherine had included specific apps and strategies that would help them effectively integrate technology into the classroom. The focus was skewed. There was so much focus on the technology itself that teachers failed to see the connection to their daily work in classrooms.

NEUROSCIENCE REVEALS THAT THE BRAIN GRAVITATES TO THE FAMILIAR, SO NEW LEARNING IS STRENGTHENED AND SUSTAINED WHEN WE MAKE CONNECTIONS TO CONTEXT, TO PRIOR LEARNING.

ADAM

During my first days as an edtech coach, my supervisor sent me a link to an article about technology-integration frameworks that mentioned SAMR and Technological Pedagogical Content Knowledge (TPACK). I was intrigued and excited to use these frameworks to guide my work. My supervisor suggested that I always include a slide showing where learning goals align with these frameworks in my professional development sessions. As I facilitated more of these sessions, the technology-integration frameworks organically became less important to the soul of my presentations. At first, I showed them where what I was presenting would fall within the frameworks. The faces in the crowd became increasingly bored by the frameworks being shown on the slides. They were chomping at the bit for me to move on to the meat of the presentations. Soon, I stopped including the framework slide. There's nothing wrong with the frameworks, I just didn't feel they were necessary to improve my ability to present and coach.

Frameworks like SAMR, T3, and TPACK are good tools for helping teachers reflect on their own practice and evaluate their technology skills as educators. However, the teachers were put off by having to hear about another edu-acronym or matrix. As an edtech coach, looking to help teachers organically integrate edtech, Adam replaced the slide with one about what students would create and produce with his ideas and strategies. This replacement slide was designed to show how this presentation fit into the context of their content and students.

This new slide eventually evolved into how apps and strategies help students engage in the 4Cs. The 4Cs feel less evaluative than the SAMR frameworks and are "students and learning focused." The frameworks feel more teacher and technology first. Fortunately for Adam, the supervisor and admin never asked about the frameworks slide again. Nobody missed the slide. The new, organic approach resonated with teachers.

For evaluating and measuring organic edtech integration, we don't recommend using the frameworks. As mentioned earlier, the frameworks are a great tool for teachers to self-reflect on their practice and edtech skills. Those reflections can be great fodder for organic edtech conversations among teachers and their coaches or administrators. From the coaching and leadership perspective, measuring meaningful, organic edtech is better measured through the lens of the 4Cs.

Since these first ineffective presentations, we do not speak with teachers regarding SAMR, T3, TPACK, or other educational technology frameworks unless they bring it up themselves. Instead, we ask a lot of questions. We engage teachers in designing lessons with a specific learning goal at the forefront. Our approach has shifted from telling teachers what they can do, to asking them what they want students to learn. Our presentations are more interactive. Each session is different than the last because it is based on the needs of those in front of us. How is this done? We lead with learning, never with tech. We tell teachers that we are tough on content but easy on delivery. We are not asking teachers to change what they teach, but how students learn. And we use verbiage with which they are familiar, the 4Cs.

– CHAPTER 9 –

4Cs LESSON DESIGN LOGISTICS

I f educational technology frameworks are not the answer, then how can edtech coaches guide educators in designing pedagogically sound technology integration that leads with learning? The answer lies in shifting the model from teachers disseminating knowledge to empowering students to own their learning. This is backed by the spirit of the International Society for Technology for Education (ISTE) standards for students, UDL, Common Core State Standards, Computer Science Teachers Association (CSTA) standards, and Next Generation Science Standards (NGSS). It also supports the skills employers are looking for. Colleges and careers call upon students to be actively engaged in their learning, to think critically, collaborate, create, and communicate. Students who engage in inquiry, research/investigation, and evaluation of content become adaptable problem solvers.

We wholeheartedly assert that all educators are doing what they believe is best for their students. However, too often we continue hearing phrases such as "I do, we do, you do," "Teachers need a textbook adoption," "I don't understand kids these days," and "I'm not good at technology." The standards are centered on students. Each of these phrases focuses on the adult first. When teachers focus on a direct instruction/textbook-centered model in which the adult or textbook company is presented as the ultimate expert and dispenser of knowledge, they inadvertently fail to prepare students for the world in which they live—and the world in which they'll work.

Educators are natural helpers. They *want* to support students. With the best of intentions, they sometimes focus on teaching students "all the answers" rather than fostering an environment in which learners experience productive struggle and grapple with content.

As edtech coaches, our goal is to guide educators toward flipping the model and placing students at the center of all we do, in a learner-led environment. But again, this shift is best accomplished organically, using a method that honors the experience and the professional autonomy of the educators plus the natural, human curiosity of the students. Otherwise, we fail to allow our adult learners to own and lead their own learning. Empowered teachers lead to empowered students. We can model this shift in our coaching. We have found that a 4Cs lesson design model is an effective way to guide teachers through this shift.

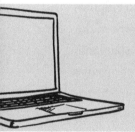

AS EDTECH COACHES, OUR GOAL IS TO GUIDE EDUCATORS TOWARD FLIPPING THE MODEL AND PLACING STUDENTS AT THE CENTER OF ALL WE DO, IN A LEARNER-LED ENVIRONMENT.

A SAMPLE MODEL

Planning with the 4Cs does not require a complicated plan or template. In designing lessons with educators, we often begin by drawing a quadrant on a piece of paper or whiteboard. The quadrant is approachable, fosters divergent rather than convergent thinking, and appears nonevaluative. The format of the quadrant is open-ended and does not feel constrictive. It is not a ladder to climb. It sparks creativity and honors educators' professional autonomy. Its simplicity is easily replicable and memorable.

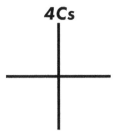

Once the quadrant has been created, ask educators for their academic learning goal. This question is the gateway toward leading with learning, not with tech. The technology integration will be natural and organic, allowing students to engage with the academic content. The academic learning goal is written above the quadrant, and then the ideation can begin. Each quadrant represents one of the 4Cs, with room to sketch or write ideas for engaging students in each.

The next step is to ask questions. As edtech coaches, be careful to allow the educators themselves to lead the planning process. Educators need to feel that they can replicate this approach when we are not present. You might begin by asking, "What are your ideas for having students collaborate as they are learning this content?" A teacher may indicate that students will speak with a partner during the process of citing textual evidence that reveals character traits in a novel. "Excellent," we may say. "This is a great way to ensure students are actively engaged in their learning."

At this point it might be helpful to say something like, "I find that when I am in the classroom with students, I want them speaking, as this is a great way for them to synthesize and reinforce their learning, but I struggle to hear all the conversations. Do you struggle with this as well?" By sharing a possible pain point with teachers, you place yourself in their shoes and provide a gateway to suggest a technology tool that can address this challenge. Typically, teachers respond to this question with an understanding comment. "Yes, that is true," they may say.

Now you've created an organic path toward introducing a digital platform for collaborative conversation. Discover if teachers are familiar with Flipgrid or Seesaw, both of which can be utilized as a digital verbal discussion platform. Next steps may be a demo lesson or coteaching. Some teachers feel comfortable trying the platform on their own.

The completed 4Cs quadrant may not look the same for each educator with whom you work. This is an organic process. Even with teachers that have the same learning goal, each individual conversation will lead to organic ideas—founded in the context of each teacher's students. This process, like all edtech coaching actions, is personalized. It honors teacher autonomy and builds upon strength.

Leading with a learning goal and not with a technology tool allows tech integration to occur naturally within the context of the learning goal first. It provides a method of engaging students in pedagogically sound methods and promotes a student-led learning environment conducted by the educators themselves. As edtech coaches, we may coach teachers with content expertise that differs from our own. Our job is not to coach to the "what" students are learning, it is to guide teachers in utilizing technology to empower students to own the "how" of the learning process.

In case of ideation struggle, try Crazy 8s to jump-start the process. We have both had the honor of becoming Google Certified Innovators and have visited Google headquarters for Innovator Academies. During these Innovator Academy experiences, we engaged in an activity called Crazy 8s. Crazy 8s is a completely paper-and-pencil activity. No tech required. Given we learned this at Google, one of the world's largest tech companies, it may seem a little out of place.

However, this is another example of the importance of leading with learning, never with tech. Crazy 8s is all about the learning. It has a low floor and high ceiling. Crazy 8s is designed to help jump-start the ideation process when engaging in design thinking. We have found that Crazy 8s a valuable activity to help teachers brainstorm before designing a 4Cs–infused learning experience. You start Crazy 8s by having participants fold a piece of paper into eight equal sections. Ask teachers to fold the paper in half three times. Unfold it and they may draw lines in the creases.

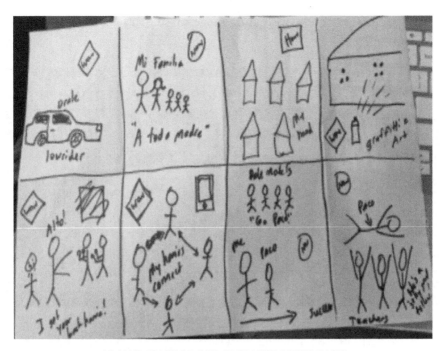

ADAM'S CRAZY 8S GRID FROM THE 2017 SYDNEY
GOOGLE INNOVATOR ACADEMY

Once the paper is set up, have them think about their goal or target and draw/write about it in the first section for twenty seconds. Every twenty seconds, participants shift to a new box where they repeat what they did in the previous box, but for a new idea. Whether they are finished with the previous box or not, when the twenty seconds are up, participants move on to the next box. Even if they had frozen and drew/wrote nothing, have them move on to the next section. The idea is that, after less than three minutes of brainstorming, they will have eight or so ideas drawn/written. Each participant's paper is now a good jumping-off point for conversations about designing a 4Cs–infused learning experience.

The 4Cs lesson design ideation process can be expanded beyond planning with individual teachers or in PLCs. We have found success introducing the strategy in professional learning workshops with educators representing various districts, grade levels, and content areas.

We begin the session with this image of students in a one-to-one environment:

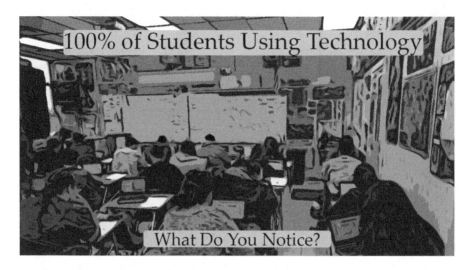

100% of Students Using Technology

What Do You Notice?

We ask attendees in the workshop what they may see that represents ineffective pedagogy. Typically, the answers we hear include: "Students aren't talking," "They look bored," "The kids aren't producing anything." This leads us to a conversation about the importance of the 4Cs in empowering students to develop the skills required by modern employers in today's world.

It is helpful to role-play what the ideation process, using the 4Cs grid, sounds like. When we facilitate a workshop like this, we ask a participant to engage in a conversation with us, as a teacher, while we model how to coach them through the process.

The next step is for attendees to work together to identify a learning goal and ideate strategies to meet this this goal with the 4Cs grid. The collaboration component is key in this process, as educators find that they build on each other's ideas and can learn technology-integration strategies from their colleagues.

The 4Cs grid process is a great way to spark ideas. However, many districts and schools require more detailed lesson plans from educators in their organization. We have designed the templates below for districts with whom we work. While these templates were created to align with specific district goals, 4Cs design is an overarching component. The first lesson plan includes links to standards and academic vocabulary. The second lesson plan embeds the 4Cs into a foundation of PLC questions and improvement science principles used by many districts in our area.

Common Core Standards (select all that apply)	Timeframe

Learning Target: Students can.......	Essential Question(s)

4Cs: How does your lesson/activity address each of the 4Cs?	
Communication	Creativity
Collaboration	Critical Thinking

Outline/Plan		Academic Vocabulary
Teacher	Student	

Assessment		
Spiral	Formative	Summative

Teacher Notes

4Cs Lesson Plan Template

1) What do we want students to learn?
• Information is available immediately with the touch of a button. How does this modern day reality affect our answer to the aforementioned question? • What must a future ready student know and be able to do?

2) How do we *empower* EACH & EVERY student in relevant learning?			
• The shift must be made from engaging students to empowering them. What pedagogical shift must occur to accomplish this end and what will it look like in classrooms?			
Creativity	Critical Thinking	Collaboration	Communication

3) How will we document the learning process?
• How do we determine effectiveness of pedagogical practices? • Do our assessments accurately depict learning in alignment to our goals for the future ready student?

4) How do we respond if students do/don't learn?
• Based on qualitative and quantitative data, what are next steps for learners? • How can we design learning environments that provide options and opportunities for all students to be successful?

We have also found the image below to be helpful for messaging where to integrate technology in the lesson design process. Educators should always start from the inside out, not the opposite way. It all begins by knowing our students: their interests, strengths, and opportunities for growth. (So once again, we are starting with "who.") Next, identify the content-based learning goals students are to learn. This is the "what." Finally, ideate and design the "how," the ways in which students will engage in the content. It is here that technology integration occurs naturally and organically, grown within the context of our "who" and "what." As mentioned before, when you plan with the 4Cs in mind, the tech takes care of itself.

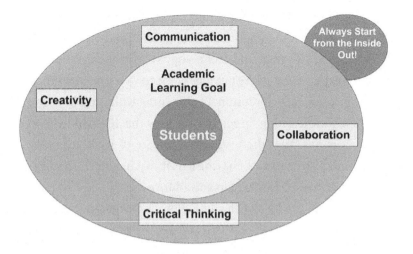

PEDAGOGICAL TOOLBOX

In 2018, Marvel's *Black Panther* took the world by storm, becoming one of the most successful box office draws of all time. One component of the movie really got Adam "EDUthinking": in the movie, the fictional nation of Wakanda was blessed with a mineral called vibranium. Vibranium, in the world of Marvel, is the strongest metal on Earth and extremely versatile. Vibranium was naturally infused into the plant life of Wakanda and it allowed the Wakandan people to develop an extremely technologically advanced society. Their technology is far more advanced than any current nation.

What really struck Adam was how vibranium was infused and integrated within all of Wakanda's technology, clothing, and lifestyle. It was not a separate thing. It was part of their lives and culture. This is a great metaphor for proper edtech integration. Too often, edtech coaches are met with resistance from teachers and admin because edtech is viewed as an extra thing, as something separate from pedagogy and lesson design. Edtech is often something on an administrator's checklist when they evaluate educators. They look for surface level usage of a device and check the box.

This is not edtech integration. Edtech, to maximize effectiveness, must be infused and integrated the way vibranium was infused into the lives, culture, clothing, and technology of Wakanda. When designing learning experiences (we're not fans of the term lesson planning), edtech can be infused, like vibranium, by designing with the 4Cs in mind.

Plan your learning target and see how the 4Cs will help meet that target. It is here that the tech will take care of itself. It is here where you'll find the true value of having a tech coach. Edtech coaches provide guidance and resources to help you address the 4Cs. Seeing the learning target through the lens of the 4Cs allows for organic, meaningful tech integration. It is this process that will allow you to integrate and infuse edtech the way vibranium was in Wakanda.

A middle school ELA/history teacher was struggling to get students to write an essay about how the Constitution helped defend against tyranny. This essay was based on analysis of primary sources from the DBQ Project. The teacher said students in years past had difficulties with analysis because they could not fully comprehend the meaning of tyranny.

To address this, we focused on the critical thinking portion of the 4Cs. We discussed ways to help students use critical thinking to develop their own examples of tyranny. We looked for ways to help students make a real-life-to-content connection to create deeper understanding of tyranny. We knew this was essential in order to get students to analyze primary sources and write the essay.

As a result of this conversation, we decided to use YouTube to show kids cartoon examples of tyranny. From there, students collaborated, communicated, and created by researching their own YouTube examples of tyranny, discussed these examples, and wrote rationales about why their chosen videos were examples of tyranny. A few weeks later, this teacher was beaming with excitement on seeing how much improved their essays were compared to years past. The essays and analysis showed a much clearer understanding of tyranny. This improvement, based in the 4Cs coaching approach, allowed the edtech integration to be organically infused like Wakandan vibranium.

At one time or another, we have seen friends and family having a good time in a swimming pool. It looks so fun and refreshing. With that in mind, you simply jump in. Often, there is an initial shock due to the water being much colder than you expected! So, you get out and rethink getting back in. You want to join in, but aren't sure you want to endure the shock of the cold water and spend the time getting acclimated to it. The pedagogy of organic edtech integration is similar. It looks so cool and cutting-edge. Your teachers, from the outside, may be tempted and intrigued, but if you lead them to jump in blindly, without taking proper baby steps, disillusionment and resistance may ensue.

In the beginning of our edtech coaching journeys, some of the best advice we received was to get on Twitter, Voxer, Google+, and Facebook to grow our PLN (personal learning network). In all honesty, this book would not have been written if we hadn't heeded that sage advice. As we forayed into Twitter, we stumbled onto edchats such as #TOSAChat, #DitchBook, #TLAP, #CAedchat, #ConnectedTL, and many more. Connecting with educators on these chats further ignited our passion for edtech integration. We had found our people. We were on fire for edtech.

Adam's fire for chats burned so brightly that he'd participated in chats while bathing his three daughters. One of these chats led him to Matt Miller's #DitchBook. This chat is an offshoot of his best-selling book *Ditch That Textbook*.

Matt Miller's *Ditch That Textbook* is catchy. He's actually not suggesting you do away with textbooks, rather that you do away with faithfully following textbooks as if they are the only road map to learning. DITCH is actually an acronym for Different, Innovative, Tech-laden, Creative, and Hands-on. *Ditch That Textbook* asserts that textbooks are just one of many resources educators should draw upon. *Ditch That Textbook* is designed to inspire educators to create relevant teaching that fosters student buy-in and an enjoyable learning experience.

This book and participating in the chat became seminal moments for Adam's edtech coaching career. Miller actually featured one of Adam's chat ideas on his blog. What a great shot of EDU adrenaline!

Miller's ideas and those of the educators Adam connected with validated his own burgeoning understanding of what he could accomplish. With validation in tow, Adam showed up to work feeling he had the ability and ideas to sustain all the initiatives, ideas, and strategies he was trying to employ with teachers.

Validation fuels our fire. It fueled Adam's to the point where he began to come across as overbearing and intimidating. Teachers initially were resistant to the *Ditch That Textbook* revolution that was suddenly taking place in their coaching time. This was completely unforeseen and unexpected. Why would anyone resist these great ideas? Why would they not want to do what's best for students? It was at this moment Adam remembered that, while validation is powerful, so is empathy.

So, he took the initial resistance as an indication to slow his roll. To think empathetically and put himself in the teachers' shoes. A concept like Ditch That Textbook, though familiar to some, was completely foreign to most teachers Adam was serving. Hitting them over the head with a slogan like Ditch That Textbook made them feel as if he was devaluing their years of experience as educators. Of course, they wanted what's best for students. They were doing that in their own fashion. Storming in like a bull in a china shop, expecting teachers to dive right into ditching their textbooks, was not the right approach.

WHEN TRYING TO HELP TEACHERS INTEGRATE EDTECH AND SHIFT THEIR PEDAGOGICAL PRACTICES, YOU NEED TO LEVERAGE THE TEACHERS' STRENGTHS AND EXPERIENCES.

Organic edtech integration begins with relationships.

From there, you show how your work and ideas will make their lives easier. Adam came up with a Ditch That Textbook spin-off called Ditch That Copier. Ditch That Copier was based on every educator's negative experiences of fighting with and for the copier. This is a common pain point among educators. Helping to solve a common problem is a great way to build a foundation for a coach/teacher relationship.

As teachers began to see how the Ditch That Copier movement made their lives easier and teacher workflow more efficient, they began to find value in edtech coaching. Adam worked on simple ways to use apps such as Google Classroom, Google Forms, and DocHub to do paperless activities and avoid the pains of the copier. Teachers saw how these ideas could enhance the things they were doing and make their lives a little bit easier and more convenient. This didn't devalue what they had been doing. The decision to change and shift was theirs.

Now they more frequently reached out for the next steps. And this foundation of small steps allowed us to implement a greater pedagogical shift . . . like Ditch That Textbook. Teachers were seeing edtech coaches not as the Google people who fix their printer, connect their projector, or set up Google Classroom. They were embracing edtech as part of pedagogy, not something separate. It's important for any edtech coach to understand that any pedagogical shift is not the first step, but the end goal. There needs to be a slow build. Without it, fire and enthusiasm for such shifts can be intimidating. To get to the goal, hands need to be held one step at a time.

– CHAPTER 10 –

EdTech Integration Strategy: Use, Remix, Create

In learning complex coding language and concepts, students first use a program (running it and analyzing the code, noting what they observe and wonder about how it is constructed). Next, students take a previously created code and remix it. This iteration and experimentation allows them to receive real-time feedback as they run the program with each altered coding command. Finally, students create their own code for a program. If students are asked to go straight to the create stage, they may struggle to know where to begin. They have not had the opportunity to experience, analyze, and rework code.

When Katherine began coaching, she asked teachers to move to the create stage right away. After starting with a learning goal, she would guide teachers in designing a technology-infused lesson from scratch. At the time, she believed that teachers needed to construct their own methods of integrating technology, that the act of creation would empower them to own the work. However, this only prepared teachers for disappointment and frustration. There is benefit to the use-remix-create model in coaching. The diffusion-of-innovation model supports this strategy. If we throw our late majority and laggards—half of our teachers—directly into creation, their anxiety level rises and their brain connects edtech with a negative experience.

KATHERINE

Kelli is a passionate teacher who loves her students and empowers them to participate in textual analysis and complex conversations about literature. She provides opportunities to engage with informational and narrative texts far above what is expected in classes of the same grade level. I loved visiting Kelli's classroom. Students actively learned and made connections from content to their lives. They left her classroom eager to continue their learning the following day.

When I began coaching at Kelli's school site, she was visibly nervous and frustrated by the idea of integrating technology into her classroom. This was openly expressed in staff meetings. After all, Kelli had been teaching for years and her students were successful learners. She told me that in her time in the computer lab, she literally got a headache. She indicated that while she understood the reasoning for infusing technology into her instruction for the benefit of her students, she had no idea where to start. It was my experience with Kelli that taught me that it is not always wise to begin with the create stage. Kelli first needed an example.

I asked Kelli for a copy of her upcoming lesson plan and resources. I spent a great deal of time creating a HyperDoc, and modeled its use with the students with Kelli observing. HyperDocs are transformative, interactive Google Docs replacing the work sheet method of delivering instruction, the ultimate change agent in the blended learning classroom. I did not give Kelli a strategy off the bat. I led with her learning goal. The process was organic. It was not a one-size-fits-all approach. Since I had spent time in Kelli's classroom as a walking coach, I knew that the learning experience I designed mimicked many of the effective collaborative, inquiry-based strategies Kelli was already using. Students used the HyperDoc as a launchpad to view videos, create maps to build context for an upcoming novel, and both communicate and collaborate on a Padlet to engage in critical thinking as they notated learnings/predictions about the literature to be read. All 4Cs were represented, and we led with learning, not with tech.

Katherine will never forget Kelli's reaction to the lesson she had created for her classroom. "This is all of the same material!" Kelli remarked. "This is my lesson, my strategies, but better! I never thought of using technology like this."

If Katherine had asked Kelli to create, even with guidance, before she had the opportunity to observe, progress would have been much slower. Instead, Kelli saw a lesson implemented that had already been created (similar to running a premade code). Next, Katherine created a second HyperDoc for Kelli. She happily implemented this on her own, with Katherine in the room in case there were any technology glitches. Once Kelli went through the use stage of the process, she was ready to remix and then create.

Perhaps the most affirming and impactful result of the collaborative work with Kelli was the way it began to influence the entire staff. As Kelli shared her experience during staff meetings, her excitement about how technology was empowering her students in the learning process was contagious, and others began to ask how they could replicate similar strategies in their own classrooms. Today, a few years later, Kelli has become an edtech leader on campus. New teachers come to her for advice on edtech integration. She is making a greater impact on the entire school campus than she may have realized was possible.

USE

Teachers often need experience observing a premade model, built organically to meet their learning goal. So we design or find a premade 4Cs–infused lesson for them. This could consist of anything from a HyperDoc, screencast example, collaborative slide deck created for a similar class, or a premade Flipgrid experience. As an edtech coach, it can be helpful to begin with strategies and technological platforms with which you are most comfortable when utilizing this process. Once the teachers have used the learning experience created or provided for them, ask what they notice and wonder about the lesson design. This provides a starting point for teachers and often sparks ideas for them to remix it to their own needs.

AS AN EDTECH COACH, IT CAN BE HELPFUL TO BEGIN WITH STRATEGIES AND TECHNOLOGICAL PLATFORMS WITH WHICH YOU ARE MOST COMFORTABLE WHEN UTILIZING THIS PROCESS.

Where Adam works, marking the text and citing textual evidence has been a huge initiative. Being an edtech coach with a Ditch That Copier mindset, and knowing the amount of paper consumed when marking text, a strategy called BookSnaps immediately came to mind. BookSnaps are a great way for students to digitally mark text, cite evidence, and be creative. (For more information about BookSnaps, go to tarammartin.com) In a nutshell, students use Google Slides, PowerPoint, or Seesaw to mark images of text.

Teachers initially were excited about this strategy, but also somewhat intimidated by the mechanics of facilitating it. To allay their fears and feelings of intimidation, Adam asked teachers send him the text they wanted students to mark, and he created BookSnaps slide decks in Google Slides for them. With the slide decks already made, facilitation of BookSnaps became more comfortable for them. Seeing this, Adam curated some BookSnaps templates on his website for teachers to easily access. Removing small hurdles like this helps teachers get on board with using tools like BookSnaps. Slowly, word spread of this new activity that meets district initiatives but is engaging, empowering, and eliminates time wasted at the copier. Now, a growing number of teachers routinely rock BookSnaps completely on their own.

If you seek solid examples for teachers at the use stage, we recommend *Ditch That Textbook*, EduProtocols, and HyperDocs. EduProtocols are instructional lesson frames designed to engage students in learning through the 4Cs, with focus on using technology to this end. This is pedagogically sound. HyperDocs, when done as intended, also lead with pedagogically sound learning.

As stated on hyperdocs.co:

A true **HyperDoc** is much more than some links on a document.

- Creators deliberately choose web tools to give students opportunities to **Engage • Explore • Explain • Apply • Share • Reflect • Extend the learning**.
- Digital **collaboration** is choreographed to give every student a voice and a chance to be heard by their classmates.
- **Critical thinking** and problem-solving skills can be developed through linked tasks.
- Students have an opportunity to **create** authentic digital artifacts to show what they know, and **connect** with a wider audience.

Each of the aforementioned resources provide multiple examples on their websites, which can be a great starting point for educators to engage in technology integration as a first step in the use stage.

REMIX

One of the most rewarding experiences for edtech coaches occurs when an educator feels empowered to own the work and remix a strategy they have introduced. The remixing process reveals that technology integration is growing organically, within the environment of a teacher's classroom. When a teacher remixes an idea, strategy, or app totally on their own, you have an organic edtech coaching win.

ADAM

Dana Jobe is a high school science teacher I have had the privilege of coaching. During an edtech coach walkabout (when I informally walk through classrooms and leave feedback), I noticed the content Dana was teaching was ripe for sketchnotes. I met with her during her prep and shared with her why sketchnoting would be a great way to engage and empower students in her science class. Dana, to my delight, took my sketchnoting suggestion and ran with it. Every week she sent me student sketchnotes to be scanned and curated on my Cardinal Innovation Center website.

Soon, Dana came to me with an idea. She had an observation coming up and wanted her observation lesson to combine sketchnotes with our district's initiative toward fostering academic conversations. Her idea was to take what I taught her about screencasting and smash it with sketchnotes. The Dana Jobe remix was brewing! She asked students go to the Sketchnotes Gallery on my Cardinal Innovation Center website and choose a sketchnote from a recent science concept. If their sketchnote was in the gallery, they were required to choose one that was not theirs. From there, students were strategically paired.

Their task was to explain the concept portrayed in the sketchnote for at least two minutes to their partner. The partner's role was to ask clarifying questions to make sure their partner spoke for at least two minutes. Before starting the conversation, they had their selected sketchnote on their Chromebook screen. When the conversation began, they used the Screencastify Chrome extension to record the conversation. This way, there was a record of the conversation and it was submitted to Google Classroom for Dana to review.

With fifteen conversations going on at once, it would have been impossible for Dana to monitor all of them. This activity would have taken multiple days if she asked each pair to converse one at a time. Her idea allowed all kids to participate in one class period, and the recordings allowed her to review these conversations more carefully and provide more focused feedback. In the end, Dana's remix was a homerun lesson for her observation.

An EduProtocol listed in *EduProtocol: Field Guide Book 2* is Sketch and Tell. According to the book, the Sketch and Tell protocol engages students in creating a visual image (similar to a digital sketchnote) of the central concept, pair-share an explanation, and then individually write an explanatory paragraph. The digital sketchnote is then done using the drawing tools of the digital platform (Google Slides, PowerPoint, etc.). Katherine introduced this strategy to teachers familiar with the strategy of drawing a picture of a sketch, and then inserting this image into a collaborative slide deck presentation using the webcam. These teachers made a connection between both strategies.

They began to remix the two strategies together, designing a new smash of ideas. In mathematics, visual representations of number sense are vital for building conceptual knowledge. Many educators prefer to have students draw these visuals on a whiteboard or create a color-coded sketch with colored pencils. Once this is complete, the students take a picture of their whiteboard using the webcam on their device, and then insert this image into a collaborative slide deck. Next, students utilize the tell and collaborate portion of the Sketch and Tell protocol. While the remix was a relatively small iteration, it offered teachers the sense that they had the power to iterate and innovate based on what they had learned.

A few days after teachers smashed the aforementioned strategies together, Katherine began to prepare a professional learning session to support English language development. The teachers' appsmash entered her mind and she remixed it to meet this new context. As a first-grade teacher, she would read a picture book aloud to her students, but would not show them the illustrations. Students sketched their visualization while listening, boosting comprehension skills. Next, they spoke with a partner to compare and contrast their illustrations, and finally they would add written text below the images.

Rather than beginning with tech tools to design the upcoming English language development session, Katherine started with a low-tech strategy. This ensured that the integration was organic, building upon the context of what she knew worked. Similarly to the way we coach teachers, to remix rather than re-create from scratch, Katherine leveled up on a foundation based on the 4Cs. The result was a four-part strategy: listen, sketch, write, respond. It does not differ much from the appsmash used by mathematics teachers; it simply adds a listening comprehension component.

Just as we ask educators to begin with one or two strategies first, and build on this foundation, edtech coaches must practice the same technique ourselves. A week after the English language development session, an English language arts coach asked for assistance providing students a way to engage with the 4Cs when pulling out the main idea from informational text.

Working with the coach, we came up with another iteration of the appsmash. Students were to become journalists reporting a central idea from an informational text they had read. They had a choice of being either an illustrator or newscaster. The strategy leverages sketching and inserting images into a slide deck, writing a caption, and responding via comments. This is nearly identical to the English language development strategy. However, it builds with an additional option for demonstrating understanding—video. Students use Flipgrid, a collaborative video platform for the same purpose.

ADAM

Recently, I had the privilege of coteaching a weeklong lesson on Medieval Manor Life in a seventh-grade class. To kick off the lesson, the teacher and I remixed and put my own spin on the Fast and Curious EduProtocol. As most of the students are English learners, developing vocabulary is a must. The smashing of Quizizz and Quizlet was a great help in doing that.

Students individually spent seven minutes on a premade Quizlet study set getting to know the vocabulary cold turkey. When seven minutes of solo practice was up, they moved into teams for three to four rounds of Quizlet Live. When the game begins, each member of the team has a few potential answers, but only one actually has the right answer. The team must collaboratively discuss the prompt or vocabulary and determine which member has the right answer and submit.

I could go into all the details of the mechanics of Quizlet Live, but what really stood out to me was the smiles on faces. This lesson took place on a Monday morning. The energy in the room felt more like a Friday. The conversations were organic and not forced. The feedback was instant and you would hear kids talk resiliently about not missing that one the next time.

This class contained a couple of students who are on IEPs. An aide was also present for additional support. The teacher and I had discussed accommodations we might need to make, and tried to plan scaffolds to help these kids fully interact in the activity. None of the accommodations were necessary. The aide stood back and let them jump in.

What was most encouraging was the looks on their faces. These are kids that often feel left out from interactive activities, but here they felt like part of a team. They felt needed and wanted like never before. Both were beaming throughout the entire activity. Other kids were psyched when they found one of these two on their teams for a new round.

In a nutshell, Quizlet Live did create a boisterous atmosphere. Not all teachers are used to that, but in this case, the learning was collaborative and authentic, and two kids who don't normally fully engage felt proud to be part of the team. My question to you is, who are those kids who might feel left out and how can you leverage tools like Quizlet to help make them smile and feel included?

As edtech coaches, we are always iterating and innovating. In continuing to remix the strategies with which we are familiar, we model continuous improvement and keep ideas fresh for those we serve. These innovations occur organically. They develop based on the needs of the environment in which we walk.

AS WE SPEND TIME, CAGE FREE, AMONG THOSE WE SERVE, WE OBSERVE OUR ENVIRONMENT SO THAT WE CAN PROVIDE CONTEXTUALIZED SUPPORT TO OUR LEARNERS.

Organic edtech coaches walk cage free. We observe environments and are among those we serve. But what does it look like? What does it mean to be a walking coach?

Many coaches ask teachers to sign up for coaching. Administrators often ask the same. While it is important to be available for sign-ups, inclusive coaches are committed to improvement and support for *every* adult learner. We often walk through classrooms without a schedule. We show up without being invited. Sign-up opportunities for teachers are by no means our primary means of support.

When you, as an edtech coach, are observant of your environment—when you walk your classrooms and engage in conversations with those you serve—you will be better able to remix ideas that may not have included any technology integration at all. As such, you can infuse technology into solid, instructional strategies that empower students to more effectively engage with content and each other. Consider the following remix, developed to meet the vision of educators in the area who seek to increase opportunities for English learners to listen, speak, read, and write.

Educators and administrators often recommend boosting communication and engagement by students through the think-pair-share strategy. While this strategy is a great start, with the potential to engage nearly all students in listening and/or speaking with a partner, it can be difficult to take records of multiple conversations occurring at once. The think-pair-share strategy can be remixed by utilizing Flipgrid or Seesaw, both of which can be used as collaborative video platforms to digitally document verbal conversations.

In our current technologically charged world, teenagers are increasingly engaged in written digital communication. We have found it increasingly vital that we provide students practice with participating in digital academic conversations. Teachers relay that students use texting language in academic papers, whether written or typed. College and career experiences of the twenty-first century extend beyond verbal conversations to include message boards, e-mail groups, threaded conversations, and other forms of digital communication. Students must learn appropriate netiquette, lest they risk losing scholarships, college acceptance, and/or employment opportunities. We have a responsibility to provide guidance and practice in safe and responsible digital communication.

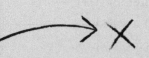

WE HAVE A RESPONSIBILITY TO PROVIDE GUIDANCE AND PRACTICE IN SAFE AND RESPONSIBLE DIGITAL COMMUNICATION.

Also, group verbal discussion skills are vital for college and career readiness. Academic conversations and Socratic seminars build these discussion skills and promote a deeper understanding of content. But what about our English language learners and students with special needs who lack the vocabulary to confidently participate in these discussions? These verbal discussions are too often overrun by a few students who dominate the conversation. Our more reserved students, who often have valuable insights to share, remain unheard.

Would it be possible to leverage technology and solve this pain point, providing each student with a voice, whether their strength is in verbal or digital communication?

KATHERINE

As it is vital to build student capacity in both verbal and digital communication, I sought a way to combine the two. I collaborated with an English language arts coach to develop a protocol I refer to as a "Socratic seminar on steroids." When I rolled this remix out to teachers, I began by asking an educator if I could try a new strategy with their students. It is vital that as edtech coaches, we are transparent. I have discovered that teachers appreciate my honesty about any untested experiment. This not only prepares teachers for the possibility of glitches, it also makes them feel more comfortable trying something new, taking a risk with a technology iteration they had not yet attempted with students.

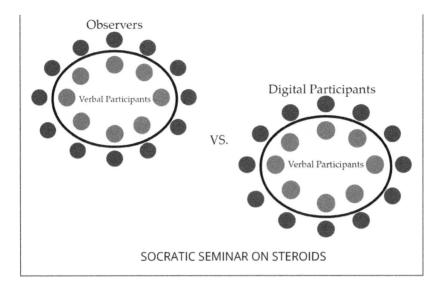

Observers

Verbal Participants

VS.

Digital Participants

Verbal Participants

SOCRATIC SEMINAR ON STEROIDS

KATHERINE

Students in the inside circle are to participate in the Socratic seminar verbally. They are not allowed to comment digitally in the conversation. Those in the outside circle are not to participate verbally. Their job is to participate in a digital back channel seen by all students. These students can ask questions of the inside circle or provide additional comments/insight. This conversational strategy is most successful when students are familiar with the topic at hand and when there are multiple valid viewpoints that could be debated. I have found that teachers who have prepared open-ended questions are able to implement this most successfully.

It is vital that students experience both the inside and outside circles. Time and again when implementing this strategy, we find that students who typically dominate verbal conversations learn to value the voices of others after they experience being in the outside circle. We also find that students who typically remain silent during verbal conversations participate at a much greater rate when in the outside circle. This fosters a culture that values variability and validates the voice of each student.

The first time I modeled this remix in a classroom, it seemed to go well from my vantage point. But the best part was the teacher's reaction afterward. "The student who was sitting here is a special needs student and English language learner. I have never seen him participate in a verbal discussion. But because he was able to listen to peers, read the digital conversation, and view the spelling/vocabulary listed, he added written insight on the digital platform. He had the confidence and scaffolds to participate."

I will never forget this conversation. As an edtech coach, the remix I had created made a larger difference than I had anticipated. The reason the remix was successful is because it grew organically based on the needs of those I serve. As an edtech coach, the better you know your teachers and learners, the more effectively you can design remixes to meet their needs. And this models a process they can emulate to create their own remixes.

In implementing the Socratic seminar, we typically use the Google Classroom stream as the outside circle's digital back channel. This stream updates in real time with the most recent post at the top (similar to Facebook). This being said, edtech coaches should be sure to utilize the platform with which our teachers are most familiar. Platforms can include Edmodo or Google Forms with a corresponding Google Sheet projected for all students to see. In professional development sessions, you can use Twitter for this purpose, with a hashtag specific for your class.

Remixes are powerful. But they must be grounded within the context of your environment. As you walk among those you serve, cage free, your ability to design organic remixes will grow. But be sure to communicate the reasoning for the remix with the teachers you serve. Let them know that it was designed with their students in mind. Edtech coaching is best approached with a personalized, context-based approach. This validates those you serve and fosters sustainability. Your remixes may look quite different from ours, but if they work with your students, empowering them to engage in the 4Cs, you know they have been effective.

EDTECH COACHING IS BEST APPROACHED WITH A PERSONALIZED, CONTEXT-BASED APPROACH. THIS VALIDATES THOSE YOU SERVE AND FOSTERS SUSTAINABILITY.

After nearly fifteen years in a district that serves mainly low SES, Hispanic populations, Adam understands the importance of making content relatable to students' personal lives and life experiences. This is much easier said than done. The important factor to realize, regardless of the demographic, is every single student has a unique life experience that should be leveraged to make real-life-to-content connections. It is in this pursuit where we can continue to iterate ideas, to remix student lives with instructional content to become what Adam likes to call hashtagged learning.

Students don't know a world without the convenience of information that is on demand and nearly instantaneous. They are used to and expect to have information, entertainment, and more on their schedules. Previous generations had to go to the library to research information. We had to make sure we were in front of the TV at a set time in order to watch our favorite shows. Kids these days don't know what that is like. Today's students are wired differently, and with that in mind, we need to rethink the way we design lessons and learning experiences.

When designing a lesson for today's kids, we must be mindful of how they will best be empowered by and engage with the content. Making the content feel relevant is a must. Instead of racking your brain to find ways to connect content with current events the teacher thinks are important, transfer that cognitive load to the students. This is where hashtags come in.

The hashtag was invented by Twitter users as a way to better search and filter topics. Think of them as labels for your tweets. In hashtagged learning, hashtags are quick forms of reflection to help students think about how what they just learned connects to their lives. Reflection and metacognition are hugely important for comprehension and authentic learning. Hashtagging your learning is a simple way to begin fostering that.

ADAM

To begin transferring that cognitive load to the students, modeling the hashtag process is essential. I like to prerecord all of my lessons and divide them into manageable-sized chunks. Each chunk is usually three to five minutes. This creates an on-demand, Netflix-type learning experience. Students are able to pause and rewind as needed and add translated subtitles if necessary.

At the beginning of each chunk, I tell them what my hashtag is. I explain what the content reminds me of from my life experience. For example, in a lesson on totalitarian dictators in a tenth-grade World History class, my hashtag was #PresidentSnow. The connection I saw was how totalitarian dictators like Stalin, Hitler, and Mussolini used similar tactics of fear and control as President Snow in Panem from *The Hunger Games*. This helped guide the kids' thinking and give them a frame of reference.

From the aforementioned lesson, some memorable student hashtags included #MyMom, #LotsoTheBear, and a variety of anime references. #MyMom is a powerful connection because these students, who are teenagers, felt their moms were sort of dictatorial over their personal lives. The #LotsoTheBear hashtag is great because the student connected a movie from their childhood, *Toy Story 3*, to what they were learning. One student, years ago, always wrote anime-themed hashtags. She loves anime and was able to connect the content to something she was very passionate about. In all of these instances, students made simple connections to the content from their own unique life experiences.

Let students know that it doesn't matter what the hashtag is as long as they can clearly explain the connection. Rationalizing the connections is where you can encourage reflection and metacognition. Experience has shown that, as students have become more adept and comfortable with the hashtagging process, many are excited to show off their hashtags and get feedback.

CREATE

As edtech coaches, our goal is to build the capacity of teachers to recognize and use solid technology-integration strategies in their classrooms, then to remix and ultimately create appsmashes and/or protocols that work best in the context of their classrooms. We inspire teachers to level up their lesson design by sharing our own stories.

THE CREATION OF NEW APPROACHES TO TECHNOLOGY INTEGRATION IS ORGANIC. IT GROWS A BIT AT A TIME.

We conclude this section with pedagogically sound examples of the 4Cs–infused experiences we have designed to empower our learners. These stories are designed to spark your imagination and inspire those you serve to level up, once they are ready for the creation phase of technology integration. Storytelling is powerful, and some of the most important parts of these technology-infused examples are our emotions during implementation, the reality of the trepidation during risk taking, and the iteration that occurs as we keep student learning forefront in our minds.

KATHERINE

Creation of technology-infused protocols are most impactful when they grow organically to meet the needs of the context of your environment. These strategies need not be complex. In working with educators of young students who had just moved into a one-to-one Chromebook environment, I recognized that educators needed a simple, replicable way of engaging their students in meaningful use of the Chromebooks each day. As I spoke with teachers and walked classrooms, I noticed that the most typical use of the devices was for learning-analytic programs (akin to educational video games). Educators needed a simple way to engage these young students in 4Cs learning. I had introduced collaborative slide decks, but some teachers struggled with sharing settings and were frustrated when students inadvertently deleted slides or portions of the template. Enter the daily writing prompt, led by an engaging animated GIF. Each day, students complete a daily, open-ended writing prompt about an image, using the create question feature of Google Classroom. The platform is simple and it prompts collaboration as students can view peer responses and ask questions about their writing. The teacher reuses the post each day rather than re-creating the assignment each time. Teachers maintain a slide deck with an animated GIF or meme per slide for each day of the school year. The reason this creation has been successful is because it was designed to meet specific needs. It is by observing our environment that we create new technology-infused 4Cs protocols, and in doing so we model this process of creation for the educators we serve.

The next level of creation goes beyond the foundation of the 4Cs to leverage the neuroscience of UDL and begins to address the International Society for Technology in Education standards for students. As edtech coaches, we continue learning. The 4Cs are infused into UDL and the ISTE standards for students. We encourage you to explore the UDL framework and the ISTE standards as well. However, be cautious about the way these are rolled out to educators. We do not want to overwhelm teachers and increase initiative fatigue. As the following stories indicate, it's better to begin learning on your own and slowly introduce the concepts and vocabulary in conversations with teachers.

ADAM

The ISTE standards for students are posted on the walls of my room. As an edtech coach, it is vital that I build my own capacity and understanding of these standards, even if I am not yet introducing them to the teachers I serve. As I am designing lessons, these posted standards often remind me of ways to infuse the concepts into the learning experiences I am preparing to model in classrooms. The ISTE standards for students are a good measuring stick for me to ensure that I am promoting technology integration that empowers students to curate and create content, promotes digital citizenship, fosters global collaboration, and provides opportunity for design-thinking principles. In debriefing with teachers about lessons they or I created, it is affirming to myself and to those I serve to point out that in addition to leading with learning and engaging students in the 4Cs, we also addressed international edtech standards for students.

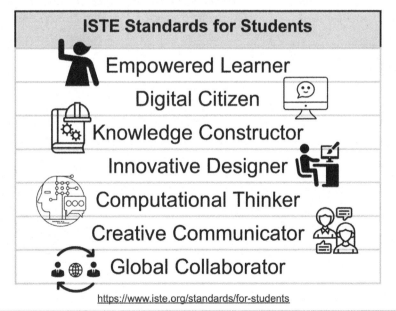

ISTE Standards for Students

Empowered Learner

Digital Citizen

Knowledge Constructor

Innovative Designer

Computational Thinker

Creative Communicator

Global Collaborator

https://www.iste.org/standards/for-students

KATHERINE

When I began learning about UDL, I began praising teachers for providing students with "multiple means of representation" of content, and "multiple means of action and expression" to demonstrate their understanding. I used the language but did not let teachers know that these phrases were from a new framework. The teachers I worked with were visibly anxious about technology integration itself, so introducing an additional framework could have put them over the edge. We continued our focus on the 4Cs, but because I began introducing UDL concepts and language, UDL did not seem foreign when it was rolled out to teachers districtwide. As an edtech coach, you can slowly pave the way to level up.

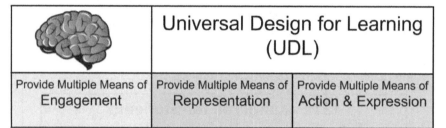

Universal Design for Learning (UDL)		
Provide Multiple Means of **Engagement**	Provide Multiple Means of **Representation**	Provide Multiple Means of **Action & Expression**

http://udlguidelines.cast.org/

The ISTE standards for students and UDL framework empower students to be resourceful, expert learners. They promote a student-led learning model in which students own the process and utilize technology according to their preferences and the needs of relevant, problem-solving tasks. But teachers worry about integrating ISTE with UDL. Will it be too complicated?

The following stories contain edtech coaching solutions utilizing elements of both ISTE standards for students and UDL principles.

ADAM

A day after teaching the basics of Napoleonic France, I wanted my history students to create something with their notes and what they learned. We'd done the whole traditional essay thing and slides presentations, but I wanted to give them some options. Enter the HyperDoc.

I created a HyperDoc with five options that students could choose to demonstrate their learning. Each option was filled with links to how-to videos and resources to add information to their project. The first option, which only allowed them to earn a passing grade of C, was to create a Google Slides presentation explaining the pros and cons of Napoleon's rule in France.

To get an A or a B, students could take those slides and screencast their understanding of pros and cons of Napoleonic France. They could also create a memes slideshow by creating a meme (with explanation) for each of the seven slides from which they took notes earlier in the week. Another option for an A or a B grade was to create a website for Napoleon's government that included his reforms and a timeline and bio of Napoleon. A fourth A or a B option was to start a blog chronicling the life, rise, and fall of Napoleon from his point of view. It would be a diary blog. I am not a huge fan of grades in the traditional sense, but it is a reality of the job. Students are programmed to believe grades are what to shoot for. So this grading system was designed to allow the students and me to live in this world, even if we were not of it.

Students were given five to seven minutes to review the HyperDoc and choose their learning-demonstration project. They were given the entire class period to get started and iterate. The project was due in ten days, but I made it clear they needed to be in constant contact with me to receive feedback.

As expected, the C option was chosen by one-third of the class, and another one-third chose screencasting. Those who chose the memes slideshow got off to a good start. Only one student chose to blog, but his first blog post was encouraging.

The example above empowers students to be creative communicators. It provides for multiple options for action and expression. It is a great start toward implementation of the ISTE standards for students and UDL principles.

– CHAPTER 11 –

EMPOWERING STUDENTS MAY NOT COME EASILY

Katherine's experience creating a student-led learning environment began with a decision to prove someone wrong. While she was in the process of obtaining her master of arts degree, a professor challenged teachers to allow students to create their own assessments. This idea seemed ludicrous. However, Katherine decided to take the plunge with a sixth-grade class for their next interdisciplinary unit, which was based on ancient Egyptian history and reading comprehension of informational text. Katherine created an academic rubric and allowed students any format they could think of to demonstrate their understanding of the items in the rubric. This experiment was so successful, it ended up transforming the way Katherine designed every learning experience thereafter. The result was thrilling! Some students created first-person narratives from historical figures, others created role-plays, and a few designed multimedia presentations. Katherine had expected this experiment in student assessment to fail. As edtech coaches, an experience like this is a humbling reminder that can help us when dealing with teachers who are also mistrustful of change.

Coaches might also find that when they flip the model and empower students to innovate, they will also encounter reluctance. As human beings, we are all drawn to the familiar. We park in the same parking spots, sit at the same seat for lunch, and we find comfort in that with which we are accustomed. Kids are no different from adults in that way.

ADAM

After I'd spent a few years out in the wild of full-time edtech coaching, my assignment changed. I'd now coach until the last two periods of the day and I would finish the day teaching two periods of history. It was in these classes where I got to really employ all the strategies and ideas I have picked up over the years as a connected educator. What I discovered was quite interesting. My history classes, as you would imagine, were very tech heavy. It was a blended model where the Chromebooks and other devices were used almost daily. At first, the kids were excited to learn in this manner. Interestingly, kids started asking me for worksheets. For them, tech was supposed to be used for fun and entertainment, not necessarily as a tool for learning, critical thinking, collaboration, communication, and creativity. A student told me, "Mister, I'd rather have the worksheet. It's just easier."

When we coach teachers to empower students to own their learning through technology, we may also be shifting the paradigm for students who have not experienced this type of environment. Teachers should be prepared for some apprehension from students. Also, as edtech coaches share stories with our teachers of the struggles we've faced in our own classrooms, we build relationships and show our humanity.

We must move toward a model that empowers students to utilize the technology at their fingertips to problem solve, create, collaborate, and communicate with others. If we simply give students the answers, we are robbing them of the opportunity to learn how to curate information and then teach others.

Many teachers provide students with a choice board of options through which to demonstrate their understanding. This is a great first step that can include options such as make a video, create an infographic, build a presentation, or build a website. However, remind teachers to always include an option that says, "or your idea."

By shifting the responsibility of demonstrating understanding to students, content-engagement levels rise dramatically and the creativity can astound us. The variety of methods students choose to demonstrate their learning also can inspire teachers to alter the way they run their classrooms. Teachers can begin to design opportunities for students to explore content on their own, and rather than being the scaffold, we guide students in utilizing tools at their disposal.

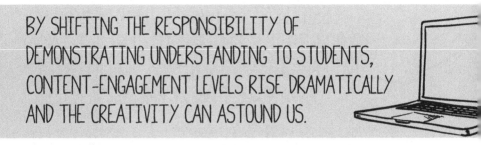

BY SHIFTING THE RESPONSIBILITY OF DEMONSTRATING UNDERSTANDING TO STUDENTS, CONTENT-ENGAGEMENT LEVELS RISE DRAMATICALLY AND THE CREATIVITY CAN ASTOUND US.

Some teachers guide students through note-taking from a textbook, ensuring that they write down every fact and concept they believe is important. However, that model places the teacher in control. Students' only reason for writing down information is because it will be on a test. The focus is on testing, not on learning.

As edtech coaches, urge teachers to focus on student learning rather than on instructional strategies. Rather than asking, "How could you teach this?" focus on students. Prompt active engagement and student-led learning by asking questions such as:

- How might we increase access to content, particularly for students with special needs?
- How might students engage in the 4Cs?
- How might we empower students to demonstrate their understanding in multiple ways?
- How might we promote problem solving and help students own their learning?

Not one of these questions mentions technology. But as edtech coaches, we can help guide teachers toward technological platforms, apps, and strategies that address these questions.

The ISTE standards for students and UDL guidelines can help frame this work toward student-led learning.

> IN ALLOWING STUDENTS LIMITLESS POSSIBILITIES REGARDING THEIR METHODS OF PROVING THEIR LEARNING OF CONTENT, WE LEARN THAT EACH OF OUR STUDENTS ARE MORE CREATIVE AND UNIQUE THAN WE HAD EVER REALIZED.

COACHING TEACHERS TO EMPOWER STUDENTS: TWO STORIES

When teachers trust students to ascertain knowledge and concepts from textbooks and technological devices, without explicit guidance, students begin teaching each other. When teachers do not guide struggling readers and English learners through each paragraph of the text, students begin using translation apps on their phones and look up vocabulary they do not know. Students begin asking questions instead of answering them. In other words, they own their own learning, led by inquiry.

Coaching Teachers

ADAM

As my district began the shift to Common Core, district administrators piloted a new Instructional Rounds process. As they implemented this process, it was a marked shift from the old way they used to visit classrooms. During Instructional Rounds, the visitors spent more time in the classroom. They no longer carried a checklist to mark what the teacher was doing. They carried a note-taking tool to chronicle what the students were doing.

For classroom teachers, this was a welcome change. The focus was on student work, engagement, and empowerment rather than what the teacher was doing and how they controlled their class. When admin debriefed with staff after Instructional Rounds, they very intentionally reminded us that the focus was on student action and work, not the teacher.

Shortly after this shift, I was hired as an edtech coach for grades 6–12. As I embarked on this new challenge as an edtech coach, the admin's reminder of focus on student action and work stuck with me and helped focus my work. Coaching a new initiative at a school site requires a strong, clear admin mandate and support. Edtech integration is no different. I chose to use the admins' focus on student work and action during Instructional Rounds to support my work with teachers. When coaching teachers one-on-one or pushed into PLC meetings, I led with the statement that admin is looking at what your kids are doing in class. This supported my coaching and edtech integration suggestions because teachers could see the students engaged in ways they hadn't been previously. They knew the admin would take notice during Instructional Rounds. As teachers began to understand that my coaching and edtech integration would help them with the Instructional Rounds shift, they opened up to more suggestions and continued coaching. Teachers shifted from trying to get admin to check things off on a list to empowering students to create and learn.

Empowering Students

Edtech coaches swiftly learn that teachers fear shifting the responsibility of learning to students. As an edtech coach, it's helpful to let teachers know that you also felt initially anxious about this paradigm's ability to empower students. This information lowers their affective filter and they are more likely to take the risk.

KATHERINE

I told the story of empowering my sixth-grade students to create an assessment to many teachers. However, those who tried it told me that the strategy did not work, that students did not know what to do with so much choice. I needed to revisit this approach in a classroom. Perhaps I had become too far removed from students, from the day-to-day experiences of a classroom teacher?

I asked a middle school mathematics teacher if I could try to replicate the strategy in his classroom. The day of my experiment, I introduced myself to the students. "I am Ms. Goyette, and I am an educational technology coach. Your teacher has told me he would like you to show him what you learned here." I pointed to a rubric created for a scaling project the students had nearly completed. I continued, "How can you show your teacher what you learned?"

As the others teachers had foretold, the students stared at me in silence. Finally, a student raised his hand. "You said you do technology?" he asked. "Well, yes . . .," I responded. "OK," he continued, "we could make a Google Doc." My first thought was, "How boring! A Google Doc? That's all you've got?" However, I wanted to validate this student. After all, he was the first student with the courage to speak up with an idea. I wrote *Google Doc* on the board. Another student suggested a Google Slideshow. I wrote this on the board.

Then I realized something. These students were not making a connection from learning strategies inside the classroom to those they used outside the walls of the campus. The examples they provided had been used in their classroom experience.

"OK," I said, "Think about this. How do you learn? Where do you go when you want to level up in a video game or learn a new dance move?" Students began to give a variety of answers, which I added to the list on the board. Examples included blogs, websites, and YouTube videos. I could have provided students with a choice board including these options, but then the ideas would have been teacher directed. When you empower the students themselves to come up with a method to demonstrate their understanding, they own the work. They are motivated. You validate them as resourceful learners and build their confidence.

As you work with educators, ensure that you continually keep student empowerment in mind as a goal. We want to engage students in active exploration of content. Keep your mind not on technology itself, but on strategies that promote communication, collaboration, creativity, and critical thinking.

HIGHLIGHT REEL: PART II

TAKEAWAYS

Lead with learning, never with tech. If teachers know their students are your priority, half the battle is fought.

- Edtech coaches can guide teachers in discovering ways to organically integrate the higher-order learning of the 4Cs via technology.

- Know the diffusion-of-innovation model, and don't expect too much of teachers too soon.

- Organic edtech integration begins with relationships—never forget that education is about people!

- Be inspired by those you serve—encourage reuse and remixing as teachers grow and learn.

New edtech approaches grow a bit at a time. That's OK—but keep growing!

QUESTIONS FOR REFLECTION

Do those you serve see you as an educator first, who leads with learning rather than tech? How might you reiterate this message?

- Consider the educators and students you serve. In what ways can you support them in integrating technology in a way that empowers students to engage in the 4Cs?

- What challenges have you faced in flipping the model to student-led learning? How can you share these stories with educators in order to promote a culture of risk taking?

BRAINSTORMING GUIDE

List ways to integrate the 4Cs:

List ways to work with early integrators:

List ways to work with reluctant integrators:

Describe a time when you led with learning, not tech. What was the challenge, and what were the results?

Think about a time when you were inspired by those you teach. How can that experience influence your work with edtech?

PART III

MECHANICS OF THE JOB

"ONE OF THE CHALLENGES OF COACHING TEACHERS IS TO GET THEM TO SEE THAT TECHNOLOGY IS NOT AN EXTRA, BUT A PART OF A STUDENT'S CORE EDUCATION."

—SARA DECUIR, EDUCATIONAL TECHNOLOGY COACH, HANFORD ELEMENTARY SCHOOL DISTRICT

– CHAPTER 12 –

FOOT IN THE DOOR

Some teachers avoid edtech coaches. They may see us as a reminder of yet another initiative. They may be fatigued with district-sponsored programs, mandates, and guidelines. The high possibility of encountering fatigued, frazzled or overwhelmed teachers makes it vital that we approach those we serve with humility, with empathy for their individual contexts. In order for change to be sustainable, we must plant seeds that are most appropriate for the environment in which we want them to grow.

As teachers, we learned that in order for an innovation to become customary in our own classrooms, the change idea needed to be flexible, adaptable, and require little prep.

WE HAVE FOUND THAT ANY NEW INITIATIVE INTRODUCED TO TEACHERS IS NOT LIKELY TO STAND THE TEST OF TIME IF IT DOES NOT ALIGN WITH THEIR WORK IN CLASSROOMS.

Edtech coaches and professional learning facilitators have discovered that implementation is most likely to occur in classrooms when teachers are provided with a limited number of ideas, complete with prep time and continued support.

When facilitating a professional learning experience, it's wise to create time within the session for educators to plan and prepare implementing a new strategy. This is best done in the classroom itself. This approach helps the innovation fit naturally into teachers' learning environments as they currently exist. It is organic. It builds upon the environment the teacher has created in their classroom. New changes that ask teachers to rethink their entire classroom routine can cause anxiety and overload. In accordance with improvement science, it is most effective to pilot incremental changes slowly. This approach is more manageable for educators and allows them to focus, to refine their practice thoughtfully.

Many educators and coaches love to use physical Breakout boxes and Sphero robots in classrooms. While engaging for students, these platforms require a great deal of preparation. The last thing teachers want to do is pile on more prep work to do. So, it's helpful to simplify the sample lessons and slide deck presentations we prepare as ideas for their classrooms. Not everyone has the skills or time to create visually stunning slides. Simple is better. Teachers need to know that the changes we suggest are doable within their skill sets—that they won't be spending hours of prep time on a single lesson. Our message to teachers is, "We are here to provide ideas that require less prep but give you more impact."

PAINS AND GAINS

As educators, there is likely one common pain point in which we all share. The copy machine. Most, if not all, educators can think of at least one horror story dealing with the copy machine. Jamming, running out of toner, waiting in line, lack of paper, and exceeding copy limits are just some of the harsh realities we face with the copy machine.

ADAM

When I first became an edtech coach, in a quest to bring value to the everyday lives of teachers, it was the copy machine pain point I wanted to help alleviate. I operated under the assumption that if I could help alleviate this pain point, teachers would be more open to edtech coaching. It helped me build trust and rapport. It was here when I developed Ditch That Copier.

Ditch That Copier sounds like a total assault on the copy machine and as if I'm suggesting you never use it. That isn't the case. Ditch That Copier is about improving teacher efficiency. Teachers whose workflow is enhanced have more time to plan empowering learning experiences. Edtech provides many options for improving teacher efficiency and workflow.

The development of Ditch That Copier coincided with an administrator mandate to "Go Google" for all staff. I was charged with leading the "Go Google" movement. Naturally, Google Classroom went a long way in helping teachers Ditch That Copier. With Chromebooks and Google Classroom numerous activities that once required hours fighting for the copier were distributed to students in seconds.

Ditch That Copier's goal was not to be paperless. The goal was to improve efficiency and demonstrate some of the value edtech coaches bring to educators. The epiphanic look on teachers' faces when they've realized the power of edtech and the value coaches provide is priceless. Adam recently helped out a teacher who normally doesn't reach out to him. They were in the staff room and Adam could hear the teacher frantically screenshotting text and pasting it into a PowerPoint. This teacher had a great activity planned for students to analyze and mark text—a great activity planned, but no time to achieve it! The teacher asked, frantically, if Adam had a quick, easy way to print thirty-page packets of text, in color, quickly before class started. Adam determined what the teacher's learning goal was and within ten minutes, they set up their Google Classroom, converted the PowerPoint to Google Slides, and assigned students to analyze and mark text using BookSnaps. The teacher was set up and ready to go with time to spare. This teacher's facial expression was priceless. Edtech coaching—and being on the spot in the teacher's environment—brought value by helping them out of a huge pinch.

Katherine has worked with a principal and her staff for the past couple of years. The staff has always been welcoming of her support and appreciative of Katherine's time guiding them in the planning phases during prep times, and providing job-embedded coaching in the classroom with students. Much of the credit for this supportive environment is, honestly, due to the support and vision of the principal, Erika Cortez. This being said, Katherine asked Cortez for her perspective on why the coaching at her site has been so well received by the staff.

"Katherine Goyette obviously has a passion for technology, and that enthusiasm **helps teachers and students see how technology can make everyone's life easier.** Not only does technology make life easier but Katherine also helps everyone see how technology makes standards easier for students to learn.

Thank you for all your help!"

—Erika Cortez, Principal, Pixley Middle School

Erika's quote addresses both pains and gains. Teachers' lives are easier via automated tasks and the management of assignments due to platforms such as Google Classroom. The teachers also recognize that technology in the classroom provides them with gains, as it builds students' access to content as they learn.

As coaches, we can add value to those we serve by focusing on pains or gains. How can we lessen pain and/or increase gain for individuals? A teacher's work never stops. They are continually seeking new ways to save time, automate tasks if at all possible, and engage their students with content.

Many educators speak of their struggle to make content accessible to students who are said to be performing below grade level expectations. This is a pain point for teachers. With positive intentions, educators often provide these students with watered-down texts, place students in remedial intervention classes to build foundational skills during core content instruction, and/or pull these students out of electives/arts courses/physical education/science for small-group reteaching at a slower pace with less rigor. However, this limits universal access and affects equity.

As educators, we are natural helpers. We want to see students succeed. It pains us to see a learner struggle. Students who are living in poverty, English language learners, and below–grade level readers often lack exposure to rich vocabulary and experiences outside of their sphere of influence. In addition, these same students often do not have reliable internet access and devices in the home. When a student misses science or arts—when they are limited to being solely exposed to texts far more simplistic than their peers' texts—the achievement gap widens and opportunities for a well-rounded education are thwarted. English language learners, students who have not been exposed to literacy at home, learners who have experienced trauma and/or struggle with a medically diagnosed learning challenge . . . these students are not unintelligent. An edtech coach can provide teachers with guidance in utilizing technological tools to increase access for these students.

In many instances, it is possible to allow for and design accommodations rather than modify expectations. Universal Design for Learning strategies, based on neuroscience, provide us with methods of increasing access via additional methods of representation of content, many (but not all) of which utilize technology. In the world of distance learning, edtech coaches can guide educators toward phone-friendly pedagogy that does not require a high amount of bandwidth or a computer. As edtech coaches, we can help educators to provide opportunities previously unavailable to the students we serve.

OUR GOAL SHOULD BE TO GUIDE TEACHERS IN INCREASING EACH AND EVERY STUDENTS' ACCESS TO CONTENT AND EXPERIENCES WITH PEERS WHENEVER POSSIBLE, NOT TO LIMIT THEM.

This is not to say that modification is not necessary at times, but too often educators forgo accommodation options and move immediately toward lessening expectations for students. This is not the teacher's fault; it may be because they are unfamiliar with the accessibility tools available. As edtech coaches, we can support teachers in addressing equity among students.

Edtech coaches can offer guidance to teachers in utilizing accessibility tools like the following:

- Tools such as the Chrome extension Read&Write simplify websites (removing ads) to support students who may be distracted by visuals and videos surrounding a text.
- Accessibility features on Chromebooks, Apple products, and within Microsoft applications can be set to allow for text to speech.
- YouTube video speeds can be slowed, and closed-captioning can be turned on (closed-captioning can also be translated into another language).
- Flipgrid and Microsoft tools feature Immersive Reader, providing speech to text features.
- Google Translate is particularly beneficial on a mobile device, as it allows students and teachers to have verbal and written conversations in real time.

A common pain point for teachers of young students is the login process. Students who are not yet reading, or are beginning to learn the alphabet, may struggle to log in to a device with a username and/or password. This pain point can be a brick wall toward any forward progress.

As an edtech coach, if we fail to address this with teachers, all else will be for naught. It might be tempting to brush off this excuse and respond to struggling teachers by informing them that other teachers are not complaining about the issue, that learners of similar ages and younger in the same district or school are finding success. However, this does little to build a relationship with the teacher and it fails to validate their experience. Instead, it is better to work alongside teachers to create login cards complete with color-coding, to be in their rooms with students as they learn to log in to their device the first time. The message is that these tasks are not below edtech coaches. We are willing to join teachers in the work, to support them even in these seemingly menial matters. And the time is well worth it.

- CHAPTER 13 -

COLLABORATION ACROSS ORGANIZATIONS

Edtech coaches work best with the support of educators across an organization. To maximize our impact, it's imperative that we collaborate with multiple stakeholders, including information technology (IT) staff members, district-level and school-site administrators, content area–instructional coaches, and grade-level teacher teams. It may also be valuable to collaborate with teacher librarians to promote digital literacy campus-wide, industry partners/local businesses who can support your students in developing career pathways, community organizations, school-site and district-level committees, and family partnerships.

As edtech coaches, we are not IT. We are educators first: it is not our role to fix computing devices or repair Wi-Fi access points. At the same time, IT is vital for us to make an impact on teachers. If the educators we serve struggle to rely on the Wi-Fi network or devices that are not kept up-to-date, it is much more difficult for edtech coaches to help them integrate technology in an organic way.

KATHERINE

I have a couple of technology coordinators/district-level administrators with extensive IT experience that I often call upon when I am looking to make teachers' lives easier. Examples may include everything from details regarding management solutions for school-issued devices to whitelisting educational websites that are blocked by a web-filtering system. Perhaps my most valuable connection with IT has been with Eric Kwong, the technology coordinator at a district I serve. Eric and I often walk classrooms together, seeking organic approaches to technology integration that work from both an IT and an educational perspective. I appreciate Eric's interest in the educational side of technology, and I learn a great deal about the logistics of the technology and of the networks themselves. As we observe the environment of the teachers we serve, our conversations organically lead to better clarity around educational goals and the logistics that will support them.

Edtech coaches often act as a liaison between the IT department and teachers. Developing a relationship with IT is extremely important. They know the technical branch of edtech. Edtech coaches know the instructional branch. It is vital for there to be a healthy connection between these branches for effective edtech integration to occur.

ADAM

It took a few years to build a relationship with IT. In the beginning, IT set up and managed all of the user accounts in our district's G Suite domain. Eventually, we developed a system wherein I managed user accounts and the dissemination of apps, access, etc. They handled the hardware and networking side. This partnership didn't happen overnight, however. To cultivate this friendship, I turned to sports. My IT director happens to be a fan of the San Francisco Giants baseball team. As a Los Angeles Dodgers fan, naturally some friendly banter developed between us. It was this banter that helped build a working relationship between us. Nowadays, we play in the same Fantasy

Football league. At work, rarely does a week go by when we don't consult each other. He keeps me abreast of all upcoming hardware and Wi-Fi issues and refers people to me for any G Suite account and instructional side issues.

Another learning experience for Katherine came after she purchased Airserver for all the teachers at her school site. This app allowed them to mirror their iPad through their computer to project for the entire class to see. Teachers could then circulate the room during instruction, walking among their students during learning rather than standing at the front of the room. A few teachers began using the app immediately. Visiting classrooms one week, Katherine noticed that Airserver was not being utilized in many classrooms. As she continued to walk classrooms each day, Katherine continued to note this trend—particularly in one hallway. Finally, she asked a teacher if there was a problem with the software. He remarked that the Wi-Fi had become so unstable that the app was rendered nearly useless. With this information in hand, further investigation led to Katherine contacting IT, which resolved the problem.

As an edtech coach, you can advocate for your teachers to the IT department. But this requires that you build a solid relationship with IT. Katherine learned that she was one of the few coaches that visited the IT office in person. Each time she visited, she would be sure to thank them for all they do before making a request or asking a clarification question. Sometimes she would ask a representative of IT if they could teach her ways to troubleshoot, which would lessen their load and enable her to provide more prompt service to teachers. IT is not an edtech coach's job. However, it is difficult to coach a teacher in utilizing technology that is not functional. The more we can learn quick troubleshooting tips, the better equipped we are to empower teachers to problem solve and attend to the academic task at hand.

COLLABORATION WITH CONTENT COACHES

As edtech coaches, we lead with learning, never with tech. Therefore, it is important that our coaching is in alignment with solid pedagogical strategies for each content area our teachers cover.

> IT IS EXTREMELY VALUABLE TO MAKE CONTENT COACHES YOUR ALLIES. COHERENCE IS KEY, WE WANT TO ENSURE THAT TEACHERS HEAR A SHARED MESSAGE IN REGARDS TO TECHNOLOGY INTEGRATION IN THEIR CONTENT AREA.

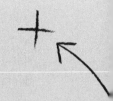

As mentioned earlier, in order for edtech integration to be organic, it must be a part of the planning stage. Throughout the year, department chairs and content coaches lead planning days for new curriculum and other resources and strategies. As an edtech coach, planning days are great opportunities to organically integrate technology. The challenge is that edtech coaches are cross-curricular. Therefore, we are not always available for scheduled planning days in individual grade levels or content areas. When this situation arises, it's a great advantage to have department chairs, grade level leads and/or content coaches who are certified in Google, Microsoft, Apple or the edtech platform your school uses.

As mentioned earlier, Adam's district superintendent made it a district goal for all teachers to become Google Certified. Administrators and coaches were expected to become certified first with teachers to follow suit shortly thereafter. In the past year, Adam has coached more than two dozen administrators and content coaches to become Google Certified. And, as a G Suite district, having coaches leading planning meetings who are Google Certified has made Adam's impact as an edtech coach greater. When he cannot be in those meetings, the certified coaches are leading the planning with an edtech lens they didn't have before. It also sets the table for more coaching opportunities, those that include deeper dives into both pedagogy and edtech.

Katherine has found it hugely beneficial to walk classrooms with content-area coaches. It always seems to spark organic conversations and lead to new ideas about how we can leverage technology to fuel academic achievement. Once, when she was walking through classrooms with an English language arts coach, they noticed that students were collecting research to be accessed later in the week for informational writing. The students were taking notes of their research findings in a spiral-bound notebook. Katherine asked the coach if there was a particular strategy students used when taking notes of their research. The coach stated that the students used a strategy called boxes and bullets. They drew a box in their notebook. A central idea went in each box, with bullets containing details to support this larger idea. "Interesting!" Katherine said, "I wonder if Google Keep could be used for this purpose." Since learning of the seamless integration between Google Keep and Google Docs, Katherine had piloted its use for research in a few classrooms. But in speaking with the content coach, Katherine was now able to attach the strategy to a term teachers heard from another coach—boxes and bullets. Now the new idea would seem less foreign to teachers. Instead of being a completely new concept, it would be attached to a context with which they were familiar.

Notice the wording Katherine used with the content coach. She did not say, "Google Keep would be so much easier!" or "Students should use Google Keep!" She also did not say, "Why are we using paper notebooks in the twenty-first century?!" Instead, her sentence began with "I wonder . . ." This maintains humility and promotes a spirit of inquiry. It invites others to consider utilizing a strategy, to decide to try something new. The language is by no means compliance based. It fosters collaborative curiosity.

COLLABORATION WITH GRADE-LEVEL/DEPARTMENT MEETINGS

In many schools, educators meet to collaborate in grade level and/or department teams to create unit plans, analyze student work, reflect upon their instructional practice, and/or prepare lessons. The presence of an edtech coach in these collaborative meetings can be very valuable to the process. But how do you join a meeting that you may not have been invited to?

Katherine has found success in bringing coffee and donuts to grade level planning days. This gives her a reason to enter the room. After delivering the coffee, she asks questions and lets the teachers know that she's available should they have any need for support during their planning.

ADAM

Getting into the PLCs is not difficult. Personally, I just walk in and observe. Making it a habit to frequently walk into PLCs, even if you just sit there and observe, makes your presence in the meeting begin to feel normal. Those times you are not there, members of the PLC begin to wonder where you are. During your frequent visits, you may get quick questions and requests. It is these quick questions and requests that lead to future invites to the PLC—and coaching invites into classrooms.

When walking into the PLCs, always leave a gift. Whether a sticky note with feedback, an e-mail or a treat, something simple goes a long way in getting invited back. Not too long ago I walked into a middle school ELA PLC. It was totally informal. I just listened and observed. After listening for a few minutes, I jotted down a suggestion on a sticky note about how the Thin Slides EduProtocol would be great with what they were working on. I handed it to the content coach on my way out. The next day, the coach called asking for more information, and invited me to the next PLC meeting to demonstrate the Thin Slides EduProtocol. That invitation led to a month's worth of in-class coaching and follow-ups.

COLLABORATION WITH ADMINISTRATORS

District- and site-level administrators can support or hinder the work of an edtech coach. It is vital that we build bridges between these positions. Teachers and students benefit when edtech coaches and administrators communicate effectively and work collaboratively to identify and solve problems.

In dialogue between administrators and edtech coaches, the role of the tech coach should be clearly defined: organic edtech coaches are not merely PD delivery bots. We are not there to report back to the admin about teachers.

An organic edtech coach will, however, keep an ongoing record of the apps, strategies, and initiatives in which they are coaching teachers. The coach's report to the administrator can be thought of as a menu of what has been coached. From there, the administrator can visit classrooms and know what to look for. The edtech coach menu approach with administrators serves two purposes:

- Making your coaching and class visits nonevaluative, and therefore more welcome. The coach is not reporting what the teacher is doing—rather, we are reporting on what we have done.
- Offering the administrator a purpose for classroom visits. In many cases it is a catalyst for administrators to spend more time visiting classrooms just to see the new stuff students are doing.

An administrator can set the tone for innovation and inspire the educators they serve to follow suit. Carole Mederos is a superintendent Katherine has worked with. Carole recognizes the potential of technology to transform learning for students, to empower learners to access and create content. At a professional learning workshop Katherine facilitated, Carole learned about an interactive presentation platform that can be used in the classroom to engage students and allow educators to view student work in real time. While Carole is the first to admit that she is "not techie," she wanted to introduce this learning tool to her district. Katherine visited Carole's campus a few weeks after the workshop.

On two separate occasions, teachers approached Katherine and indicated that Carole had used the technological platform she had learned in a staff meeting. There were some glitches, and it did not run perfectly. Carole modeled risk taking for her staff: in moving outside of her own comfort zone, she encouraged her teachers to do so as well. "Now I can try to use technology in the classroom without fear," one said. The teachers now felt that if they took a risk to use a new strategy or tool, their superintendent would support them and celebrate their willingness to innovate.

THE TEACHERS NOW FELT THAT IF THEY TOOK A RISK TO USE A NEW STRATEGY OR TOOL, THEIR SUPERINTENDENT WOULD SUPPORT THEM AND CELEBRATE THEIR WILLINGNESS TO INNOVATE.

Adam's direct supervisor is the director of curriculum and instruction. This recently hired director made it point to collaborate with him on the format and setup of their monthly district C and I meetings. This new supervisor came to Adam and made it clear she is "not good with tech" but is committed to learning. She wanted the monthly meetings to be a way for her to learn and showcase new ideas, apps, and strategies to the district's coaches and administrators.

Before each meeting, she and Adam pregamed by deciding what the focus of the meeting would be and how to use edtech to help facilitate the meeting. To date, they have used tools such as Pear Deck, Google Classroom, Flipgrid, and more to facilitate the meetings all the while exposing coaches and administrators to the empowering possibilities of edtech. After having Adam hold her hand the first few meetings, the supervisor felt empowered to plan the meetings on her own. On a few occasions, she screenshared with him on Google Hangouts for a walk through some of the setup, but for the most part, it was all her.

This method made the edtech organic. The apps and tools weren't taught in isolation, rather, they were taught in the context of the meeting. The edtech helped attendees engage with the data and reflect in ways most had never before seen.

Just as organic edtech coaches walk among those they serve, it can be helpful for administrators to do the same. Katherine's current administrator, Dr. Jen Francone, not merely observed, but participated in a great portion of an edtech workshop Katherine facilitated for leaders. Jen did not have a judgmental vibe. Rather, she was there to provide feedback and to learn. As a result of this experience, she took the learning and applied it to the creation of a website to house the employee handbook. The digital handbook increased efficiency for Jen and also for her employees.

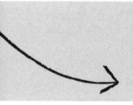

JUST AS ORGANIC EDTECH COACHES WALK AMONG THOSE THEY SERVE, IT CAN BE HELPFUL FOR ADMINISTRATORS TO DO THE SAME.

As edtech coaches, we can support all in our midst. It is not merely educators and students that can benefit from our coaching, but oftentimes administrators as well. Seek out collaboration with your leaders! A strong relationship between edtech coaches and administrators strengthens the positive impact for all stakeholders in the organization.

- CHAPTER 14 -

TECH-HESITANT TEACHERS

As a coach, you may have a couple of cheerleaders, fans who are eager to try to implement the strategies you introduce to teachers. It is affirming to work with these educators. These are the intrinsically motivated teachers who thank you for coming into their classrooms. Their faces light up when you arrive and they offer stories of how they have implemented the tools and/or strategies you have taught them. They ask questions as to the next steps in their learning journey.

Many coaches and educational leaders indicate that these are the educators you should work with first. The idea is that as coaches, we build leaders who can teach their peers, and spend our valuable time with those who want to be coached. However, there are dangers to using this as your sole strategy. It has the potential to damage the culture of a staff. When only the innovators are coached, we may create an environment in which there are two classes of teachers, the successful and the struggling. In our experience, the aforementioned model leads to a perception of the "techie" teachers, and those that are "not good at tech." This inhibits personal growth and implies that either teachers have a talent for tech proficiency, or that they will always struggle.

It takes courage to work with tech-hesitant teachers. It requires that we step out of our comfort zone and approach those who may not be interested in the support we provide. But we are called to serve people, not technology.

As edtech coaches, we love the haters. We do not avoid teachers who do not want to work with us or who say they hate technology. Just as teachers need to meet the needs of each and every student in the classroom—not just those who want to learn—we must also be inclusive in our approach.

This is a matter of equity. If a kid is in the class with a teacher who does not work with an edtech coach by choice, while the teacher next door seeks and received support on a continual basis, this is not fair to that student and all others in the class. This is not to state that edtech coaches need to spend equal time with each teacher, but that we should provide organic, personalized support to each and every educator in our midst.

When we focus just on the innovators, we widen the gap. What if we did this in the classroom? What if we taught only those who sought our feedback?

AS AN EDUCATOR, WHETHER IT IS OF ADULTS, CHILDREN, OR TEENS, IT IS OUR JOB TO FIND A WAY TO REACH EACH AND EVERY LEARNER.

The same is true in our jobs as edtech coaches. It is not always easy, but it is the right thing to do. As edtech coaches, we are called to support *all*. Edtech coaching is an inclusive sport.

While we believe it is vital that all educators receive coaching, compliance models are not sustainable. As edtech coaches, we want to send the message that we are on the same team as teachers. We are not evaluators. We are here to support. We have found success in reaching tech-hesitant teachers by focusing on elements Daniel Pink describes in his book *Drive: The Surprising Truth About What Motivates Us*. Pink states that in order to foster intrinsic motivation in those we serve, there must be three elements: autonomy, mastery, and purpose.

Organic edtech coaching meets all three factors of intrinsic motivation. A tech-hesitant teacher will not remain intrinsically motivated without professional autonomy. The minute we tell teachers they must utilize technology in a specific way, we fail to allow their integration to grow organically. If any change does occur, it will not be rooted in personal ownership of the technology implementation. When we provide autonomy for teachers, we validate them as instructional designers and send the message that we trust their ability to make decisions for the benefit of the specific group of students they serve.

Many tech-hesitant teachers are fearful of technology integration because they do not have confidence in mastery. Edtech coaches are, ideally, guides for these teachers, building their capacity to utilize and leverage technology—one platform, app, device, or tool at a time.

A tech-hesitant teacher may not see the purpose of technology integration. That is why we lead with learning, not with tech. And we start with "who." It is vital to listen to the teachers we serve, that we uncover their individual passions. Then we help teachers tap into that passion, that purpose, with the support of technology.

AUTONOMY

It is important that we are clear on our intent. Teachers must know that we are not there to ask them to throw out the great things they're doing. In walking classrooms as cage-free edtech coaches, we observe the environment and compliment those being served. We honor their professional autonomy by seeking opportunities to magnify their strengths. If coaching is organic, it provides educators with choice. There is no one-size-fits-all approach. Edtech integration does not look the same in each classroom. Organic edtech coaching never mandates that all teachers use a specific tool. Options are essential. The 4Cs lesson design (discussed in the pedagogy section of this book) honors the autonomy of educators. Autonomy overcomes tech-hesitance.

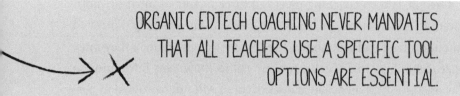

ORGANIC EDTECH COACHING NEVER MANDATES THAT ALL TEACHERS USE A SPECIFIC TOOL. OPTIONS ARE ESSENTIAL.

ADAM

To foster autonomy, I focus on building teacher skill toolboxes. For myself and the teachers I serve, I want to be as device, app, and strategy agnostic as possible. I want my teachers to have an extensive repertoire of skills and tools so they can adapt to the learning goals of any lesson and learning needs of any student.

In the past few years, I have had the privilege of coaching Diana Robinson. My first encounter with Diana was marked by frustration. During a whole-staff Google Certification PD I facilitated, she felt overwhelmed. Seeing that, and going forward, I made it a point to have one-on-one coaching sessions with her. It was in these one-on-one sessions where I helped her fill her toolbox with a variety of strategies. At no point did I mandate her to implement any strategy. I challenged her to remix what I taught her to meet the learning goals and student needs.

Diana and I are now at the point where she comes up with the ideas and asks me for lesson feedback. Not too long ago, she messaged me excited to share some student data. One of the strategies I shared with her, and she remixed, was BookSnaps. For an entire semester, she used BookSnaps as a method to help students identify textual evidence, close read, and analyze text. She was extremely proud to show me the growth nearly all of her students demonstrated. The moral of this story is that Diana felt she had the autonomy to find a strategy and run with it. Her implementation of BookSnaps was completely organic.

PURPOSE

This is not about your purpose; it is about the passions of those you serve. How well do you know the educators you serve? What do they love to teach? What is a strategy they love? What brought them into education?

KATHERINE

One day I walked into the classroom of a high school history teacher during his prep period. His administrator had asked me to support him in integrating technology. This teacher was not on board with having a Chromebook cart in his classroom for student use. When I entered the room, I introduced myself and asked for an upcoming student learning goal. Remember, edtech coaches lead with learning, never with tech. Instead of an answer, the teacher provided a barrage of excuses as to why he did not want technology in his classroom. I listened patiently. It would not have been productive to respond to each excuse. The last thing we need to do as edtech coaches is argue with the educators we serve, especially upon first meeting them. This rarely results in changed attitude or behavior. The goal is to create a relationship and foster intrinsic motivation.

Upon finishing the monologue on the dangers of technology, the teacher said, "I have heard that Google Forms will grade a quiz auto-matically for me. Can you show me how to do that?" He handed me a piece of paper with recall-level questions. I do not believe that mere memorization of facts is a pedagogically sound method of learning, but I showed the teacher how to create a form with automatic grading. Meanwhile, I was observing the environment, looking for this teacher's passion and purpose. Surely, he entered education for a benevolent reason. It is vital we assume positive intent.

I noticed that the walls of the classroom were covered with maps. "Do you enjoy geography?" I asked. The teacher's eyes lit up. "Oh yes," he answered. "It is so important that students learn geography. It serves them in understanding history and current events too! I make copies of the maps for students as we learn about historical events, but it is so difficult for them to see and manipulate in black and white." I had identified this teacher's purpose. He had a passion for geography. "Have you heard of Google MyMaps?" I asked. "No," he replied.

The remainder of this teacher's prep period, five minutes or less, was spent guiding him in designing and empowering his students to create interactive digital maps that aligned with historical content. He asked where he could find more resources like this, and when I left the room, this teacher continued through his break to explore Google MyMaps. He was intrinsically motivated to learn on his own because the technology integration aligned with his purpose.

Do not lead with your own purpose—take the time to build organic relationships. Get to know those you serve. Walk among them. Engage in conversations. Be observant. This is how you help uncover their purpose, and increase your ability to tap into this purpose to foster intrinsic motivation.

MASTERY

So many educators say, "I'm not good with technology." Educators that do not feel capable of mastering tools and/or platforms for technology integration will not be intrinsically motivated. Edtech coaches have a myriad of opportunities to support teachers that lack confidence in technology use. Remember, organic edtech coaching rejects a one-size-fits-all approach. The stories offered here reflect methods we have used to build educator confidence and help them feel capable of mastery. But always keep in mind that relationships with those you serve will guide you in determining the best approach for each teacher.

It can feel overwhelming to support teachers in ways that meet their individual needs. However, technology can help us be quite efficient. The English department at a school site Adam works with was eager to empower their students to write for an authentic audience by creating blogs. Some of these teachers asked if Adam could come into their classrooms to get students started on the platform, to model the process.

This was exciting, but it would be physically impossible for one person to model the process in multiple classrooms simultaneously. But the last thing Adam wanted to do was kill the department's enthusiasm. Instead, he recorded a video tutorial for students, via screencasting. Screencasting is a powerful tool, enabling us to be in more than one place at once. It duplicates our support! Students in many classrooms viewed the screencast tutorial he had uploaded onto YouTube. The teachers did not need to know how to use the tool or to be "good at technology." The students utilized technology to access or create content, and the educators begin to realize that they themselves did not need to be experts.

THE TEACHERS DID NOT NEED TO KNOW HOW TO USE THE TOOL, OR BE "GOOD AT TECHNOLOGY." ←

The first year Katherine moved from a single school site to many, she discovered that she was no longer able to provide on-call, in-person support to the educators being served. However, between Katherine's visits, a few educators refrained from any technology use. They'd say, "I forgot how you said to create an assignment in Google Classroom," or "I was afraid I'd mess it up so I decided to wait until you came back." In order to provide real-time support, Katherine utilized screencasting to create video tutorials and placed them in a shared Google folder. Some educators, however, had trouble locating this shared folder. So, Katherine next decided to house all tutorials, resources, and videos on a single website. This proved a much more successful method. At their leisure, educators can peruse the website or search for a specific resource/tutorial.

Since Adam became a Google Certified Trainer in 2017, he has coached eighty-nine teachers to earn Google Certified Educator Level 1 status. Seeing the sense of accomplishment on an educator's face when they pass this test is intoxicating. This exam is no joke. It is quite rigorous. Seeing the clock count down while navigating multiple choice questions and performance tasks is a little nerve-racking.

Adam has noticed some trends in people's responses to the exam. One common response is "I didn't know I could do that with Google. I am learning so much." This expression has led Adam to tell teachers the best way to prepare for the exam is to take the exam. Pass or fail, those who take the test learn a great deal. And if someone fails, they've learned something and can easily retake. That's not failure. Adam has noticed that most people who retake a second time pass the exam.

Another expression edtech coaches often hear is "I am totally going to try that in class tomorrow." As mentioned earlier, people learn a bunch during the exam. It spurs their thinking and gets educators to come up with ways to apply their learning to their classrooms immediately.

The best response comes after they've passed the exam. "Adam, when do I get to do Level 2?" This is a powerful statement because it speaks to the capacity and confidence built by passing the exam. These small wins build upon themselves and fuel teachers to seek further professional learning on their own. As educators, it's our job to learn, and the learning is much more valuable when it's something we are intrinsically motivated to do.

Encouraging certifications such as Google Certified Educator Level 1 is a great way to help educators build mastery and a sense of confidence. From there, with that sense of mastery and confidence, edtech coaches have an opportunity to empower teachers with the autonomy to innovate and develop their purpose, their "why."

While certifications and screencasting are tremendous tools for edtech coaches to design resources that build the capacity of educators, students themselves are very resourceful and can often build their own learning. Teacher expertise in technology is not necessary. Adam's and Katherine's personal learning network member and mentor Jon Corippo states, "You want tech support? You have thirty students in your classroom." Jon tells the story that when he was preparing to guide students in using Final Cut Pro, major updates to the program had occurred just before school began. Instead of panicking, Jon put the students in charge. He asked them to search YouTube for the most helpful tutorials on the software and recent updates and thereby created a classroom resource bank that would guide their learning.

Building the capacity of educators to utilize and implement edtech is key for promoting mastery. However, it is also reassuring to send the message that educators do not need to have all the answers in regards to technology. When educators flip the model and put students in charge of learning, they shift from the "expert" with all the knowledge, to a facilitator.

WHEN EDUCATORS FLIP THE MODEL AND PUT STUDENTS IN CHARGE OF LEARNING, THEY SHIFT FROM THE "EXPERT" WITH ALL THE KNOWLEDGE, TO A FACILITATOR.

Katherine's son, Dillon, is in a school that has implemented UDL, which calls for multiple means of action and expression. As such, educators empower students to demonstrate their understanding of content in the method of their choice. In his freshman year English language arts final, Dillon's assignment was to select a couple of texts read throughout the year, identify a common theme, and cite evidence of literary elements that supported the theme. Dillon was in a video production course and has an Adobe Premiere certification. He chose to complete the final by producing a video using Adobe Premiere.

Dillon's teacher is probably not proficient in utilizing Adobe Premiere. But that is of no consequence. Educators who consider themselves "not good at technology" can nonetheless empower students toward meaningful technology use. Intrinsic motivation calls for mastery, but mastery in flipping to a student-led approach, in providing choice, can also result in effective technology integration as well.

CLASSROOM MANAGEMENT/OFF-TASK CONCERNS

Many educators are fearful about student technology use due to concerns about potential off-task behavior, opportunities for cyberbullying, and unsafe online content. As edtech coaches, it is important not to dismiss these concerns as inconsequential.

If educators feel we are shrugging off their apprehension, we are not meeting them where they are. And why would they want to approach us again? Psychological safety is of key importance.

Katherine used Edmodo as a teacher to engage students in digital conversations with each other. As an edtech coach, Katherine later encouraged one of the teachers she served to use Google Classroom for a similar purpose. She helped this teacher set up her classroom and first assignment, which the teacher planned to introduce to students the following day. Katherine later visited the teacher's classroom and inquired as to the success of the lesson. "I'm done. I'm not using it again," the teacher exclaimed. Katherine asked, "What happened?" The teacher stated that students had used the platform to have off-task conversations.

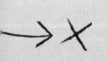

> WHILE WE MIGHT NOT AGREE WITH EDUCATORS' CONCERNS, IT IS VITAL THAT IN BUILDING RELATIONSHIPS, WE LISTEN BEFORE RESPONDING.

Any edtech coach's first instinct might be to remind the teacher that there's always a need to talk to students beforehand about appropriate comments on the platform, or to state that other teachers did not have this problem. But this reaction would do nothing to build a relationship. Instead, Katherine offered to add an administrator as a coteacher in Google Classroom. The administrator wrote a post in the classroom stream: this post expressed excitement that students would be using the platform to share their learning, and also contained a reminder that all comments needed to be kind and on topic. This simple solution helped the teacher feel comfortable moving forward with technology integration. If a student got off topic, all the teacher had to do was remind the student that the administrator could see everything posted, and the student went right back on task.

When supporting hesitant teachers, programs like GoGuardian have been immensely helpful. Teachers' fear of students using edtech to head off-task and be disruptive is real. GoGuardian allows the teacher to see what every student in the room is doing on their devices. Rules can be set on what apps or web pages kids can be on. It's a powerful tool for keeping kids on task.

When Adam's district got GoGuardian, his opportunities for edtech coaching increased. GoGuardian allayed some tech-hesitant teachers' fears, and they became more comfortable with the tech and open to coaching. Teachers who never used the Chromebook carts before were now using them daily.

– CHAPTER 15 –

THE WALKING COACH

A s walking coaches, it is our job to be proactive, to roam our environment cage free.

Edtech coaches do not wait for our phones to ring or for questions to come in our in-boxes. It is our job to find ways to reach each adult learner. To do this, we must walk among them, observe the environment, engage in the work with them. Job-embedded support is key.

Teachers may experience anxiety as we arrive in a classroom. Initially, they might not want us there. The last thing they want is another thing on their plates. But they soon realize that our approach is not to complicate their lives, but to make the learning environment more efficient. We let teachers know that our focus is "less prep, more impact." We want teachers—particularly those who are hesitant—to know that we are not there to make their jobs more difficult.

As a walking coach, be prepared for some deer-in-the-headlights looks. Adam once walked into a classroom where the teacher immediately asked if he was there to evaluate them. There are two ways to manage deer-in-the-headlight responses like this:

1. Be very intentional to work with administrators to be sure that teachers understand evaluation is not the job of an edtech

coach. If the administration can disseminate that message, you're less likely to have such a response.

2. Give advanced warning. Adam normally schedules two-week blocks where he walks classrooms for one department/subject. He creates a promo video and e-mail explaining when he will be coming and that he is there to merely observe. These are his fly-on-the-wall promos.

Since employing these techniques, the deer-in-the-headlights looks have virtually ceased.

Previously, we talked about how lonely it can be as an edtech coach. Adam often remembers his loneliest moment as an edtech coach. He sat in his office with the door locked, watching YouTube videos all day because he wanted to see if anyone would notice. That experience made Adam become a walking coach. He had to grab the job by the scruff of the neck and get out into classrooms. Being visible, in classrooms, made the job not so lonely. Immediately, opportunities to coach vastly increased.

He thereafter attended a coaching training led by then-consultant Laura Gonzalez. Laura, now superintendent of Woodlake (CA) Unified School District, challenged Adam to be in classrooms at least 80 percent of his day. This challenge (much easier said than done) reaffirmed the importance of being a walking coach. To this day, whenever Adam's in a coaching rut, he resolves to get back into classrooms as much as possible.

Katherine was provided with an office in her first year as a coach. The summer before this new role began, she spent a few days in the office decorating, organizing, and preparing for how she would use the space. She prepared for staff meetings and for meetings with teachers to offer support and organize curriculum. It made sense to be in the same location most of the day, to ensure that the educators would be able to find their edtech coach if needed. Just as Adam had, Katherine quickly discovered that teachers did not seek her out in the office. Something had to change.

It is difficult and intimidating to increase time in classrooms during the instructional day—if you haven't prepared the ground for it. It is one thing to support teachers as they plan, to provide professional learning or lead a staff meeting. It is quite another to enter a teacher's classroom when they have a full class of students in the room. In ditching the office to view learning in action, an edtech coach will sometimes encounter resistance. Some teachers may ask if you need to speak with a particular student, others become visibly nervous when you enter the room, a few may ask to fix their projectors or make copies that they had not had time to make. Katherine learned the hard way—she had failed to communicate her intentions in entering classrooms. As you make the shift toward being in classrooms on a consistent basis, let teachers know that you are there to watch students learn, not to watch them teach. This lowers the affective filter.

WALKING COACH TIPS

Focus on Student Learning

As you begin to increase your time in classrooms, focus on student learning rather than teacher instruction. When Adam and Katherine walk classrooms, they take pictures of student learning as often as possible. Rather than seeing the purpose of academic activities as merely showing compliance, students begin to look forward to these visits and show off their learning. Students and parents alike love to see learning in action, documented via images and videos posted on school social media channels. With this approach, student time on task has risen considerably. This also helps to foster collaboration among teachers.

Organic edtech coaches document student learning and then share documentation freely to prompt collaboration among those they serve. In taking pictures of student work and inserting them into a "Jefferson Journal" (a fitting title for Jefferson Elementary School) for teacher in-boxes, Katherine witnessed educators asking each other about the strategies they saw used in the images. These organic conversations between teachers were far more valuable to them than any that can be initiated by a coach. But only a walking coach can take pictures of student learning. You must be present in classrooms. If the positive impacts on students and teachers were not enough, consider the boost to your personal health. Step counts per day go up, you'll receive an increase in vitamin D by having more time in the sunlight, and you'll benefit from interactions with others.

BUT ONLY A WALKING COACH CAN TAKE PICTURES OF STUDENT LEARNING. YOU MUST BE PRESENT IN CLASSROOMS.

Adam has developed a reputation among students. They know, if he is in their classroom, that Adam will be taking over-the-shoulder pictures of their work. He always asks students if they mind him tweeting images of their work. More often than not, they excitedly oblige. Within minutes, Adam's phone begins to blow up with likes, comments, and retweets. It's powerful to go back to those kids and tell them that "so-and-so" from "somewhere far away" is admiring their work. The sense of pride and empowerment these kids get from knowing their work is being recognized far beyond their small town is priceless.

Observe the Environment and Respond to Needs

When edtech coaches walk the environment, when they are observant, they are able to identify needs and respond appropriately. This is an organic approach.

After these observations, you may identify a need to be a liaison for teachers, to IT, and/or administration. But in order to provide this support, you must be there. Presence and visibility build trust with teachers and also gives you evidence that you can show to those who can support teachers with infrastructure, equipment purchases, etc.

CONVERSATIONS AND PD ALONE DO NOT BUILD EMPATHY FOR YOUR TEACHERS. IF YOU WANT TO AFFECT POSITIVE CHANGE, YOU MUST JOIN TEACHERS IN THE CLASSROOM.

Katherine recalls walking through classrooms at a school site she serves. She noticed that YouTube was on the shelf as a shortcut on each student Chromebook. This was the case in nearly every student Chromebook in all primary classrooms. In conversations with teachers, she learned that the logo was a temptation for these students, and many found it difficult to resist the urge to visit YouTube for entertainment purposes during learning activities. The teachers had not realized that this shortcut could be removed, so they had never asked IT to remove it. Because Katherine had observed the environment, she was able to respond to a need that would not have come up in conversation. As edtech coaches, our lens may lead us to be able to make an organic change to the environment in a way a teacher may never have known was possible.

Any football fans out there? If so, you may have heard the term bump-and-run coverage. For the layman, it's a strategy used by defensive backs to cover wide receivers. Defensive backs purposefully, at the line of scrimmage, bump the wide receiver to slow them down, change their route trajectory, and gain on-the-fly insight on where they are going.

Bump-and-run coaching is somewhat similar. It occurs when you purposefully or by chance bump into a colleague in the hall. A conversation ensues about a cool idea you have for a lesson in their class, or perhaps you are able to provide them with some quick, informal support. Bump-and-run conversations often lead to coaching opportunities. These purposeful encounters require a little bit of planning on your part. Knowing where you might be able to bump into teachers is a must. Often, teacher workrooms, the office, and outside the staff lounge are perfect places to might "bump" into a teacher.

Once, after a meeting with the leadership team, Adam happened to bump into one of the art teachers in the hallway. Earlier in the year, they had collaborated on a method to use Google Hangouts and Chromebooks to help students see demonstrations better in a large classroom setting. This collaboration made the teacher comfortable seeking support and coaching from Adam. In this chance encounter, the teacher had a technical question about how to bypass the firewall so she might access certain art websites that were blocked. Adam knew a hack. She was grateful, and, not too long after, she came to Adam for training on the Google Certified Educator Level 2 exam—and passed.

Scheduling Tips to Foster Mobility

Scheduling tool use can help you keep up with your daily grind. Adam is a vocal advocate of keeping his day on track with a few tools and tricks.

ADAM

I try to be in classrooms at least 80 percent of my day. Maintaining my schedule is essential to this approach. As I am in a G Suite district, I use many Google tools to keep me organized. Depending on your district's platform, there are plenty of options for accomplishing what is described here. Google Calendar, Google Keep, and Google Tasks help me make sure I know what I have to do and where I have to be. Google Calendar is a very robust, yet easy to learn tool. A popular feature among coaches is the Calendar appointment slots. In my experience, adding the school bell schedules has been a great Google Calendar trick. Adding school bell schedules require a little bit of work to set up, but once you have them in, planning in-class coaching with teachers becomes much easier.

Most schools don't have a bell schedule that can be imported directly to your calendar. This is true of the schools I serve. I manually input these schedules into Google Calendar. The first step is to create a separate calendar for the bell schedule and add all the class periods to that calendar. To expedite the process, become a master of the repeat function in Calendar. This allows you to create a class period once and repeat it for the entire school year.

After inputting all the repeating class periods into the bell schedule in Google Calendar, scheduling with teachers becomes a breeze. If I want to coach a teacher who is teaching third period, I no longer need to know the exact beginning and ending times for the period when entering this coaching session into the calendar. All I need to do is open the third period event and duplicate it. I then edit the duplicate with the teacher's name and the purpose for the coaching.

Remembering to schedule teachers is a job for Google Tasks. Often, as a walking coach, during those bump-and-run moments, things get scheduled informally. I use Google Tasks to jot down the teacher's name and other relevant coaching information. I add a reminder for later in the day to add this teacher to Calendar.

Google Keep is useful in managing to-do lists when coaching multiple school sites. What I need to do at one site is usually very different than what is needed at others. To this end, I create separate Google Keep notes for each site. I use the location-based reminder function to have this note pop up on my phone each time I arrive at that school. This has been invaluable in increasing my efficiency and improving workflow.

In working with multiple school sites, Katherine found that it was important to have touch points in between visits. So, she looks at her calendar often and schedules follow-ups on specific dates. If she doesn't create a note such as "E-mail first-grade teachers from Wilson School" a week after a visit for follow-up, it is likely to be forgotten. In the e-mail, she may thank teachers for welcoming her into their classroom, celebrate a success from the previous visit, and let them know she looks forward to working with them again on a particular date. In Katherine's work as a business owner before her career in education, she often heard the phrase "the fortune is in the follow-up." It is vital to have these touch points, reminders of our presence to those we serve. But scheduling them is key.

Be Mobile and Accessible

Office staff and teachers need a way to contact you outside of your office. There are many steps you can take to be sure you are always available for those you serve.

- Forward phone calls from your office to your cell phone.
- Encourage office staff to text you.
- Set up notifications for e-mails on your smartphone and/or smartwatch. Many leaders use a platform such as Google Hangouts for chat, Voxer (walkie-talkie app), or Slack.

Also, consider answering e-mails and completing logistical work in classrooms. Keep in mind, you may need a privacy screen. Students walking by may look at your laptop when you are viewing sensitive student information. As you begin this strategy, start with teachers with whom you have developed trust.

Google Hangouts is a video conferencing and instant messaging app developed by Google that has gone through several iterations. Just now, Google is getting ready to phase out the classic Hangouts we've used for years in favor of separating the chat and video call functions into separate apps (Hangouts Chat and Hangouts Meet).

Adam feels that Hangouts is an app that has been far underutilized. It was slow to catch on with the one hundred fifty teachers and administrators he serves. But now the Hangouts buzz in his district is growing. If you're looking to expand use of Hangouts with educators and students, here are some ideas he has used to get people onboard.

Remote Tech Coaching

As a tech coach who serves three school sites, Adam cannot be everywhere. Often, he is called for quasi IT help as educators need assistance figuring out where to click or how to find a file. Driving across town to support them is not always feasible. Google Hangouts (or similar platforms) can be leveraged to solve this through video call and screen-share functions. On many occasions, Adam's supervisor needs help as she seeks to integrate more tech into her PDs and meetings. Recently, she needed assistance with setting up grids and topics in Flipgrid for her monthly curriculum and instruction meeting. Adam could not meet with her in person, but he was available to assist her via Google Hangouts. She was able to share her screen with Adam, and he guided her through the process of setting up her Flipgrid.

Adam also has used Hangouts integration with Google Calendar to create a standing, weekly event where teachers can ask questions and he can offer tips remotely. Adam invites all staff to the event, and all they need to do is open that event in Calendar and click the video link to call from the comfort of their classrooms.

Be Forgetful and Unforgettable

In our experience, we have found that there are a couple of great ways to get into classrooms as a walking coach. This is to be both forgetful and unforgettable.

ADAM

Being forgetful is a trick I stumbled onto inadvertently. I have a photographic memory, but at the same time, I am absentminded. Go figure. When on coaching walkabout, I am usually armed with my phone, tablet or laptop, sunglasses, and coffee mug. When I walk out of a classroom, I often forget my sunglasses or coffee mug. This absentmindedness has created a measure of edtech coaching serendipity.

I get phone calls, texts, and/or e-mails from teachers saying I left something behind. I go to retrieve my belongings, but it is in these return trips to the classrooms that organic edtech coaching opportunities take place. I get questions for support. They pick my brain for ideas. Often teachers tell me that, during my initial visit, my presence gave them an idea and they couldn't ask for feedback during the flow of the class. My absentmindedness gave them the opportunity to have that conversation. Instead of being embarrassed about my absentmindedness, I now embrace it. When I leave things behind in a classroom, more often than not, it is done purposefully to elicit that phone call, text message, or e-mail to come back.

There's an old cliché that says the fastest way to a man's heart is through his stomach. We like to say that the fastest way to a teacher's heart is through their students. Katherine has found this to be true. In her work with a couple of high school teachers, she facilitated a UDL lesson in classes where students would select their method of demonstrating understanding of content. Katherine informed students that she knew they would produce creative, impressive products, and that upon her return a month later, she would create a digital portfolio via a website to showcase their work. On a rainy, dreary day one month later, Katherine walked onto that campus again. One of the students from this class saw her and exclaimed, "You're here today!" She gave Katherine a hug and continued, "I made some slides for the project. They even have some memes on them that I made. Are you making the website today?"

This student's excitement shows us the impact that we can have as edtech coaches, as we guide educators to empower students to use technology. And student excitement also speaks to the educators whom we as coaches serve. When the teachers saw the pride on their students' faces when their work was showcased on a website—they were sold. One teacher created her own class website during a break. When we become compelling for students, the teachers want us to return and empower them yet again.

> WHEN WE BECOME COMPELLING FOR STUDENTS, THE TEACHERS WANT US TO RETURN AND EMPOWER THEM YET AGAIN.

Being unforgettable is also an opportunity to be a little silly. Having fun and inserting some silliness into the grid of school is a great way to break up monotony. It also helps make learning memorable. As edtech coaches, demonstration lessons are a part of what we do. The trick is to make those demos memorable to the point where kids ask the teachers to bring you back, or to do more of what they learned with the edtech coach.

One simple way in which Adam inserts some silliness into a demo lesson is to bring a bag full of funny hats. He arrives armed with blond wigs, farmer hats, a panda hat, rainbow beanies, and more. He tells the kids they may wear the hats while they work, but they have to stay on task in order to keep wearing them. Admittedly, in some classes, Adam has had to shut the hats down, but for the most part, it livens the atmosphere and engages the majority of students. Adam also pledges to take a whole class selfie with everyone wearing their hats—if the learning goal is met. Otherwise, no selfie.

Soon thereafter, students would see Adam around campus and ask when he was coming back or if he could teach their teacher more fun edtech things. He told them to ask their teacher. As mentioned earlier, the fastest way to a teacher's heart is through the kids. It's a lot easier for a teacher to tell an edtech coach "no" than to say that to their students.

Create a System for Follow-up

When you are visible on campus, educators, staff, students, and parents may approach you with concerns or questions. Be sure to have a method of taking note of these conversations so that you are able to follow-up. Currently, Katherine and Adam both use Google Keep, which features location and time-based reminders. Automating note-taking and reminders using AI (make Siri, Google, or Alexa do it!), gives us more time to invest in building personal relationships. It is difficult for all of us to remember the details of conversations we've had throughout each day, but everyone who approaches us deserves a thoughtful response and follow-up if needed. We show that we value those we serve by ensuring that their concerns will be met with a response. If an edtech coach does not have a system for follow-up, stakeholders will stop approaching us. Relationships and the culture of the school will suffer.

Feedback While Walking Classrooms

As mentioned earlier, when walking classrooms, you should always leave a gift. That gift should be the gift of feedback. Even if you had no edtech suggestions, a simple sticky note with praise goes a long way. Adam borrowed an idea from his PLN member Ben Cogswell, who was nice enough to share a template on Google Slides that creates custom sticky notes. Adam put his Bitmoji on his personalized sticky note, along with a speech bubble and contact information. He's received nothing but positive responses as he leaves these sticky notes on each classroom visit.

Katherine often leaves a Post-it or two celebrating something she observed, or an idea in the form of a question such as "Have you considered color-coding digital slides for students to match the anchor chart I see on your wall?" and a smiley face with the words, *Have a great day!* When a teacher sees this custom Post-it note, a headshot instantly reveals who left the note to ensure that they know where the feedback is coming from. The Post-its also list Katherine's website address, which can lead teachers to additional resources.

It also can be a good idea to have your Twitter handle on the Post-it. Why the Twitter handle? It can be the quickest way to reach someone. Katherine answers e-mails, but not nearly as quickly as tweets in which she's tagged, or a direct message (DM) on Twitter. This has another benefit: it encourages educators to use the platform to become connected educators. By being welcomed to the Twittersphere and reminding them of that space on each Post-it, educators are more likely to remember our conversations about the resources available on this platform.

The Post-it also encourages us to be concise. It's easy to be long-winded when we are passionate about something, but teachers are busy. They need to be provided with feedback and support in small chunks, increasing the likelihood that they will read and recall the notes.

IT'S EASY TO BE LONG-WINDED WHEN WE ARE PASSIONATE ABOUT SOMETHING, BUT TEACHERS ARE BUSY.

Katherine was in a classroom a couple of weeks ago and walked to the teacher's desk to leave a Post-it as normal. She smiled as she noticed that the note of encouragement she'd left previously was still there. Want to personalize your feedback to teachers? Discover the power of a Post-it. And, when you can, draw a smile at the bottom of each message.

KATHERINE

As an edtech coach, I love to automate tasks. I love that thanks to technology I can walk into a classroom with a phone or tablet in hand and fill out a digital feedback form that is instantly e-mailed to the teacher when I click Submit.

A few years ago, I overheard one of my teachers remark to a colleague from another school site, "When Katherine is in my room, I get an e-mail right away when she walks out the door. It's like magic!" Technology can make our job seem magical. It gives us the cool factor as we implement tools that those we serve have not seen before. When I first started using this automated feedback form, word spread quickly across the district. Principals and coaches contacted me wanting to learn how to implement this system themselves. Our superintendent raved about how we used the spreadsheet of results collected from the form to create instant charts and graphs with the click of a button.

Before entering any classroom, we review our own digital notes from previous visits. With more and more teachers, it becomes increasingly difficult to remember exactly what had previously been observed and how we provided support.

One of the tools we use for automating our feedback is a Google Sheets add-on called FormMule. You start by creating a Google Form to collect data and jot notes or feedback. In the form, you must have a place to select or enter the teacher's e-mail address. Once the form is created, set the form to collect responses in a Google Sheet. In the connected Sheet, go to FormMule and you can set it where on the moment you click Submit on the Google Form, the notes and/or feedback you typed are automatically e-mailed to the teacher. Go to bit.ly/tcjformmule to learn how.

– CHAPTER 16 –

EdTech
Coaching Vehicle

As an edtech coach, a vehicle to guide your work can prove impactful. An edtech coaching vehicle is a mechanism, physical and/or virtual, that curates the work done as a result of your coaching. It also inspires and empowers teachers to improve their professional practice.

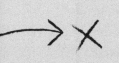

AN EDTECH COACHING VEHICLE ALLOWS YOU TO CARRY INSPIRATION TO THOSE YOU SERVE, TO TRANSPORT KNOWLEDGE AND SPARK INNOVATION IN CLASSROOMS.

As organic edtech coaches, we transmit examples of pedagogically sound technology integration, led by learning, never by tech. Our edtech vehicle supports educators and students while serving as a conduit for building educational technology proficiency and confidence.

Katherine's and Adam's edtech coaching vehicles are quite different from each other. And as an edtech coach, your vehicle may contain components of ours, or not. What matters is not the vehicle itself, but the way it is developed, with an organic approach that meets the particular context of your environment. Below, we reminisce on how they organically developed their individual edtech coaching vehicles:

ADAM

#CanICICIt

Cardinal Innovation Center

The Cardinal Innovation Center is both my edtech coaching vehicle and Google Certified Innovator Project. It was born on my daily commute. Every morning in the car I brainstormed ways to improve my effectiveness and prove my worth. The very first incarnation of the Cardinal Innovation Center came from the fleeting idea that I could pull the "kids that got it and needed a challenge" out of class so the teacher could intervene and remediate with kids who needed support in a smaller class setting. This first step in building an edtech coaching vehicle started with five seventh-grade biology students. They had just learned about biomes. The teacher intervened with the remainder of the class on the concept of biomes while the five students "who got it" worked with me, in my office, using tech to take their understanding of biomes to a new level. They wrote a blog, did green screen news reports from each biome, and posted screencasts on YouTube. When they returned to class a few days later, they trained the rest of their classmates on some of the tech tools and strategies they learned with me.

After this first successful test run of my coaching vehicle, the next step was to upgrade my office to a student-centered learning space. I ditched my desk, added a ton of whiteboard space, and made the furniture more comfortable and flexible. I then developed a website (cardinalinnovationcenter.org) to curate the artifacts and work kids created. A few months later, I inherited a new, larger room at our high school and was donated thousands of dollars of whiteboard walls, two seventy-inch TVs, and Apple TVs. With my good friend and colleague Ed Campos, we put casters on the desks to make them flexible and mobile (all for under $300). (Adjustable desks with built-in casters often cost $300 each!) The Cardinal Innovation Center was beginning to take shape. It became the go-to location for PD. Kids asked their teachers when their classes were heading to the Cardinal Innovation Center.

After a year of development, the idea became my Google Innovator Project. My edtech coaching vehicle is designed to be a space that empowers learning and is a model for student-centered learning. Using it, teachers have gleaned ideas, bits, and pieces from the Center, and upgraded their learning space to use tech and the 4Cs more effectively. Anytime someone asks, "What is your impact as an edtech coach?" I simply guide them to my edtech coaching vehicle, both the physical room and the website. It is tangible evidence of my work. My vehicle was developed out of the circumstances unique to my job, school, district, and community. The Cardinal Innovation Center is a model, but *not* a blueprint. When developing your own edtech coaching vehicle, take into account your unique situation. Think of the teachers and students you serve, the budget available, money you're willing to invest (I invested a lot of my own money), relationships with administration, and your time.

Adam's relationships with administrators is strong. There is a clear line of communication and when they see the work kids do as a result of his coaching, they get behind Adam's ideas. Also, through his extensive PLN, Adam was able to procure some generous donations and win a small cash prize for his idea as 2017 LeRoy Finkel Fellowship Finalist at CUE. Don't read this and think you need to design some amazing learning space to be a great edtech coach! Adam did because his circumstances allowed it. But, at the very least, you can create a website, blog, or some place to curate the work done by kids as a result of your coaching. The most love comes from any place where your coaching has resulted in curated student work and teacher ideas.

KATHERINE

A few years ago, I had the great privilege of taking on a leadership role at a school situated in a neighborhood with a poverty rate at three times the national average. I had done a great amount of research on the digital divide, and the students I served reflected these statistics, with relatively low rates of technology access and use at home and in school. In my first year at this site, we increased access to devices and created schedules to provide equitable opportunity to the technology across grade levels and classrooms. However, implementation of effective technology integration was not easy.

I needed a learning-led vehicle to drive technology integration. And I wanted it led by those who would benefit the most, our students. Tiger Tech Team began as a student-led technology club, designed to increase campus-wide technology proficiency to empower learners. The students even came up with the name! Tiger Tech Team student leaders managed a website and blog, tutored younger peers, and while Tiger Tech Team increased technological proficiency on the campus and in the surrounding community, perhaps the most rewarding result was the leadership development of its members and their impact on school culture. Tiger Tech Team facilitated cross-age tutoring relationships, built pride in the school, and gave students an avenue to make a difference in their community. It also increased teacher confidence in implementing technology in the classroom. Students teaching students. Learners becoming leaders.

Unanticipated challenges arose along the way. As an instructional leader, I had often preached the power and importance of student-led learning and of student choice to teachers. Again and again I asked them to allow students to struggle before providing them with assistance, to move away from direct instruction to a model in which students own the learning. Initially, students were not comfortable with this shift.

In time, the student tech team stopped asking me for direction to guide their work, and began owning the vision. These students became observant learners of their environments, telling me stories about family members who needed to learn how to fill out job applications online and peers who struggled to use web tools effectively. The work grew organically, according to the needs of the environment. The Tiger Tech Team members' emerging leadership became a catalyst for positive change. Leaders created learners who in turn became leaders themselves. And as student technological proficiency increased, teachers were more willing to integrate tech into their school day, to take risks in trying new tools, confident that student leaders would be available to help troubleshoot technological glitches. Tiger Tech Team resulted in greater technological skills on campus, but its largest impact was on the pride it has helped to create for the campus and surrounding community. Tiger Tech Team was never about the tech. It was about creating leaders of learning.

Both Adam's and Katherine's edtech vehicles were built around the circumstances and needs of their students. Your edtech vehicle can and will be equally successful, provided it is created organically around your school environment.

HIGHLIGHT REEL: PART III

TAKEAWAYS

Share common pain points to connect with teachers' challenges.

- To succeed, new initiatives must align with the teacher's goal in the classroom.

- Edtech coaches work as a collaborative hinge within the school, connecting administration, IT, departments, and classrooms.

- Edtech coaching is an inclusive sport: embrace your tech-hesitant teachers.

- Flipping the classroom model toward student ownership can fuel learning for students and teachers.

- An edtech coach must be in the classrooms. Job-embedded support is key, and only a walking coach can observe and respond.

Powerful edtech coaching vehicles develop organically, led by the needs of both students and the community.

QUESTIONS FOR REFLECTION

What is your foot in the door with those you serve? What organic edtech coaching strategy might you add to your toolbox?

- Consider the stakeholders that may support your work as an edtech coach. How might you build a collaborative relationship with these individuals?

- Do you walk your organization cage free? How might you increase your time in classrooms, with educators and students?

BRAINSTORMING GUIDE

List pain points that teachers share:

List three ways you can be more of a walking coach:

List ways to work with reluctant integrators:

List a few successful student-led classrooms you've seen or implemented. Then list a few unsuccessful ones you've seen. What signaled the difference between success and failure?

In what ways must your edtech coaching vehicle be unique to serve the specific students and teachers you work with?

PART IV

PROFESSIONAL/
PERSONAL GROWTH

"EDUCATION IS A COLLABORATIVE SPORT."

—JOE MARQUEZ, CUE DIRECTOR OF ACADEMIC INNOVATION

– CHAPTER 17 –

FEED YOURSELF TO FEED THE TEAM

Everyone who's flown in an airplane recalls the quick preflight presentation about what to do in case of a plane malfunction. The flight attendant makes it a point to remind passengers to put on their own masks before assisting others. If you fail to put on your mask first, you may pass out trying to help that person.

This is a great metaphor for much of life—and particularly organic edtech coaching. As an edtech coach, putting on your oxygen mask first means taking the initiative to learn the latest apps, strategies, and tools before bringing them back to the students and teachers you serve. With your mask on and the edtech oxygen flowing, you can better serve the various edtech, pedagogical, and learning needs of those you coach.

To this end, we encourage you to build a personal learning network, both online and in-person. Earn badges, certifications, and build competency in as many topics as possible. Become device, platform, app, and strategy agnostic.

CERTIFICATIONS AND BADGES

As an edtech coach, certifications and badging serve multiple purposes. Firstly, the professional learning expands your knowledge base. It also builds confidence and increases your clout among administrators, teachers, and students.

The districts we serve utilize G Suite (Google Suite of Apps for Education). Based on this context, upon being assigned to our edtech coaching roles, we each studied independently and took assessments to become Google Certified Educators. While completing the certification assessments, we learned new aspects of the platform. We were hooked, and moved on to Google Certified Educator Level 2 and later, Certified Trainers and Innovators.

Edtech coaches are not perfect. We do not know it all. Learning is a process, not a destination. During the journey toward earning Google Certified Trainer and Innovator certifications, there were bumps in the road. Each of us were rejected for the Google Certified Innovator program the first time we applied. It is human nature to feel dejected at moments like this. If this (or something like this) happens to you, we urge you to continue on the journey. Continue to learn and move forward. Reach out to colleagues and mentors to iterate on your applications for your next attempt at the Innovator Academy. We cannot do this job alone.

While our districts utilize Google, we also sometimes receive questions regarding Microsoft Office and Apple platforms as well. Consequently, we sought out additional certifications and became Apple Educators and Microsoft Innovative Educators. In the process of taking the assessments, we continued to learn. We built our toolbox to better expand our ability to design organic experiences that leverage learning for students. And the more we have in our toolbox, the better our ability to meet the organic needs of those we serve.

Once you have learned a new strategy—once you have added to your own toolbox—find a way to implement the strategy in your context as soon as possible. This cements the learning and strengthens it through an application.

Katherine learned the no-tech ideation strategy called Crazy 8s during the Google Certified Innovator Academy in Toronto. This strategy for divergent thinking leads to ideation driven by time limits. Constraints increase creativity, and the strategy's requirement of sketching eight ideas in only twenty seconds each leads to innovative, atypical solutions. Upon returning from the academy, Katherine quickly used this process in network meetings, professional development sessions, and in her own creative work as an edtech coach. This strategy employs the use of paper rather than devices, but it has proved to be effective in promoting divergent thinking for ideation of innovative edtech solutions that meet the needs of stakeholders. And this no-tech strategy reiterates the fact that we are educators first, and a technology integrator second. As always, we lead with learning, not with tech. Crazy 8s can be used in a multitude of settings. This learning was sustained because Katherine applied it as quickly as possible in the midst of her role.

Sustainability of skills and strategies is essential to organic edtech integration. As mentioned before, no one person can be an expert in all things edtech. Edtech moves and evolves very quickly. Staying up-to-date and maintaining skills is pivotal, and earning certifications and badges can be extremely helpful. Earning badges and certifications might remind you of the badging process seen in the Boy Scouts and Girl Scouts. Scouts wear their badges proudly. Each badge tells a story of proficiency. Badges and certifications beget other badges and certifications. This creates a personal culture of sustained, professional learning.

STAYING UP-TO-DATE AND MAINTAINING SKILLS IS PIVOTAL, AND EARNING CERTIFICATIONS AND BADGES CAN BE EXTREMELY HELPFUL.

While obtaining certification for our own professional learning is a key to success as edtech coaches, it is even more rewarding to inspire and support those we serve in achieving their own certifications.

> "Working in a district that provides edtech coaches has been amazing for teachers and students. I have not only become Google Certified, but I have also been provided with many different tech strategies and sites to use within the classroom. The ability to work side by side with an edtech coach has built my confidence in accessing technology within my classroom and utilizing technology within my core curriculum lessons. Student engagement has definitely increased due to the amount of technology used. This generation may be tech savvy, but providing them with the different tech resources to keep them organized and becoming college and career ready has made all the difference in their lives."
>
> —Michelle Cruz, Third-grade teacher,
> Golden Valley Elementary School, Orosi, CA

As Google Certified Trainers, we have helped facilitate the Google Certified Educator Level 1 exam for hundreds of teachers. Seeing the sense of accomplishment on their faces when they pass the exam is a wonderful thing. Almost immediately, we get questions about prepping for the Level 2 exam, and they cannot wait to post their Level 1 badge on social media and e-mail signatures. Going through the Google Certification process, and that of other platforms, is like scout badging for educators in edtech.

To maintain Google Certified Trainer status, we are required to take a skills test annually, in addition to logging trainings. Those who earn Google Certified Educator Level 1 and 2 certificates must recertify every few years. The recertification process is rigorous, but the maintenance of the certification is important. It's not something educators like to lose, so they keep learning and their toolkits keep expanding.

ADAM

Certification brings a measure of clout to your job as an edtech coach. It breeds confidence in your skills among those you serve. Early in my journey as an edtech coach, I was given a clear mandate by administration: lead the district's transition to G Suite. To this end, I dove in headfirst with Google Certifications. Like those I now coach, when I passed the exams, I was excited to share my accomplishments with staff. I quickly became known as the "Google Guy."

Riding a wave of confidence after earning the first two Google educator certifications, I successfully applied to become a Certified Trainer. As an edtech coach, the clout I received from admin upon earning the Google Certified Trainer certificate was a huge shot in the arm. Administration made more of an effort to support edtech integration, knowing they had a Certified Trainer on board. This support got me thinking about ideas for a Google Certified Innovator project.

One morning, on my daily commute, my Innovator project, the Cardinal Innovation Center, was born. Excitedly, I applied for the 2017 London Google Certified Innovator Academy. I was not accepted. Undaunted, I applied for the 2017 Sydney Academy and was accepted. It was one of the proudest days of my career as an educator. One of the principals I serve, Roberto Vaca, was over the moon excited for my accomplishment. He took me out to celebrate and also gave me carte blanche to redesign a classroom, hardware, and autonomy to implement my vision of organic edtech integration with teachers regardless of department.

When the 2017–2018 school year commenced, I had two shiny, prestigious certifications in hand, Google Certified Trainer and Innovator. Word of my success filtered its way to our superintendent, Yolanda Valdez. Seeing how Google certifications empowered me, Mrs. Valdez set a district goal of all teachers and administrators becoming Google Certified Educator Level 1.

The mandate was given for me to lead the training and professional development for meeting this goal. Ambitious as this goal is, it required more than my expertise. The superintendent herself made it a point to become one of the first to become Google Certified Level 1. From there, nearly all of the administrators followed suit and slowly but surely teachers were becoming certified.

This story is not meant to shed light on Adam's accolades, but to reveal how the clout of certifications and badging creates sustainable opportunities for coaching. Without Adam becoming a Google Certified Educator, Trainer, and Innovator, the district goal set by the superintendent may not have occurred. The certification and badges earned were a great advertisement for edtech integration. With these wheels in motion, and dozens of teachers now certified, Adam's ability to organically integrate edtech has greatly increased. Teachers and administrators, due to their confidence using G Suite and other edtech apps, better understand other edtech ideas when they receive further, organically integrated, coaching.

– CHAPTER 18 –

CONNECTIONS >
INDIVIDUAL KNOWLEDGE

Educational technology iterates quickly. There are thousands of apps, multiple platforms, and new start-ups creating tools on a continual basis. Because of this reality, we have found that the edtech community is very connected. Connection is a necessity, in fact, for expanding our knowledge and resourcefulness.

> WE CANNOT KNOW THE INS AND OUTS OF EVERY TECHNOLOGICAL TOOL IN EXISTENCE, BUT WE CAN BUILD A NETWORK OF INDIVIDUALS TO REACH OUT TO FOR SUPPORT, EACH OF WHOM HAVE A SPECIALTY WE CAN LEVERAGE.

Continually feed yourself via connections. Networks will grow organically as you seek additional knowledge, and prove to be powerful for professional learning. Personal Learning Networks can seem complicated, but as you'll see in the story and image below, social media can be the fastest way to pick up valuable tips, tricks, information and updates. An edtech coach is always learning.

— KATHERINE —

A colleague of mine, Janell Miller, tagged me in a tweet asking about an augmented reality (AR) tool. While I am aware of apps to recommend to get teachers started with AR, I am by no means an expert. However, I knew that fellow edtech coach Joe Marquez—who I had interacted with via educational Twitter chats—had used AR quite a bit. I tagged Joe in an answer to Janell's Twitter post and she received an answer a day later. Joe also tagged the Twitter handle of the company whose app he recommended. They then replied, offering to provide support. It sounds complicated, but here's how easy it looked!

Joe Marquez, The EdTech MacGyver ⌄
@JoeMarquez70

Replying to @IamJanellM and @kat_goyette

If you want to try something a little different kids can create #VR galleries of their work with @cospaces_edu Ss can have own accounts

8:23 AM · Sep 29, 2017 · Twitter for Android

4 Likes

💬   ⟲   ♡   ⬆

CoSpaces Edu @CoSpaces_Edu · Oct 2, 2017 ⌄
Replying to @JoeMarquez70 @IamJanellM and @kat_goyette
We're here and happy to help anyone that wishes to get started with #CoSpaces 😊

💬 1   ⟲   ♡   ⬆

Janell Miller @IamJanellM · Oct 2, 2017 ⌄
Just put on my phone. Does it work with iPads? Are cardboard glasses needed? Will uploaded images work for objects?

💬 2   ⟲   ♡ 2   ⬆

6 more replies

Katherine Goyette @kat_goyette · Sep 29, 2017 ⌄
Replying to @JoeMarquez70 @IamJanellM and @CoSpaces_Edu
Nice! Can't wait to look into this more. Thanks!

💬   ⟲   ♡ 1   ⬆   ٜ||ٜ

In Adam's early days as a coach, "Flipgrid Fever" began to spread. At the time, he had heard of Flipgrid, a video-based platform for collaborative conversations, but had not used it much. Teachers began asking him about it. In an effort to help teachers eager to learn about this application, Adam turned to his PLN. The great part about building a comprehensive PLN is that if there is a topic or app in which you are not an expert, someone out there will be! Even if your PLN is still growing, thoughtful inclusion of applicable hashtags can result in answers from educators with whom you have not yet connected.

In Adam's quest to learn more about Flipgrid, he tweeted his good friends at #TOSAChat (Twitter, Mondays at 8:00 p.m. Pacific) and #CVTechTalk (Twitter, Wednesdays at 7:00 p.m. Pacific). Adam also

Adam Juarez
@techcoachjuarez

Ok #PLN I just got a subscription to #flipgrid & I know nothing about it. I need your best tips, tricks and ideas. Go! #cvtechtalk #ISTE17

8:39 AM · Jun 16, 2017 from Orosi, CA · Twitter for Android

2 Retweets **14 Likes**

Adam Juarez @techcoachjuarez · Jun 16, 2017
Replying to @SelmaEdTech
Yes

2 1

Efraín Tovar, M.A.Ed 🍎 @efraintovarjr · Jun 16, 2017
Let's meet up

1

1 more reply

Joe Marquez, The EdTech MacGyver 🖋📗☀ @... · Jun 16, 2017
Replying to @techcoachjuarez
I Got you!!! Let's meet up! #FlipgridFever

1 1

included the hashtag #FlipgridFever. As you'll see, Adam asked if anyone could send him resources and ideas regarding Flipgrid best practices. Very quickly, his PLN stepped up with more ideas than he'd anticipated.

Adam took Sean Fahey's advice and reached out to Karly Moura. She then sent along a treasure trove of resources to get started with Flipgrid. Evan Mosier's tips were also very helpful. Since this experience, Adam has spread Flipgrid fever throughout the schools he serves. It has become commonplace to see students in his district sitting outside their classrooms with Chromebooks, recording their responses to teacher prompts, using the Flipgrid platform.

These experiences prove the power of a PLN. As educators, we don't have to be an expert in all things. In fact, it's impossible in the rapidly evolving field of edtech. A PLN connects us with those who are experts and can help us best serve the needs of our students, teachers, and admin.

COMBAT LONELINESS: BUILD YOUR PLN

"Having a PLN makes you a better teacher because you can get so many great ideas from teachers in other places. It makes you realize that we are all struggling with similar issues in the classroom and makes you feel supported."

—Jessica Reed, MA, SPED teacher from Alabama

The job of an edtech coach can be lonely for a variety of reasons. At times, you feel as if you don't belong anywhere. Edtech coaches support educators across disciplines and/or grade levels. And although an edtech coach may have experience in a few of these contexts, they are nomadic when it comes to being a member of the departments and PLCs on campus.

Oftentimes—particularly initially—when edtech coaches are conducting a coaching walkabout, teachers view them as an administrator who has come to evaluate. They may react defensively with a comment such as, "Oh, I'm not doing tech today." Reactions like these make edtech coaches feel unwelcome in classrooms.

Edtech coaches can also feel lonely when administrators view them as PD delivery machines. This leads to days of preparing slides and PD sessions in their office, as opposed to walking classrooms and working with teachers and students.

Early in Adam's edtech coaching journey, he was excited at the possibilities of his new job and giddy about all the cool apps on which he could train teachers and students. He expected teachers to be just as enthusiastic as he was—that his phone would ring off the hook and his in-box would blow up with edtech coaching requests. Reality was a different story. No one called, and his in-box was dormant. He couldn't understand why teachers were not reaching out.

Adam sat in his office and waited.

ADAM

At my lowest point, I decided to do a little experiment. Would anyone notice if I was not around? I locked the door to my office and sat inside all day watching YouTube videos. I was certain that someone would come looking for me. Lo and behold, I watched YouTube videos all day without a single interruption. Needless to say, it was a lonely day. It was then I resolved to take matters into my own hands.

To combat the loneliness, I decided to be a walking coach, to build relationships and be among those I serve. I knew I had to be visible to teachers and students. But I also knew I would need support. I needed to further develop my PLN to include edtech coaches who could support me in this endeavor. Soon, I attended a session at a local edtech conference facilitated by my longtime friend and mentor Jon Corippo (@jcorippo). Jon gave me the best, yet most simple advice I've ever received. He told me to get more involved on Twitter. He said the experts on Twitter are giving away their knowledge for free. He said to connect with them and not to be afraid to reach out to them. And it made a world of difference. In fact, the Twitter platform is where Katherine and I had our first interactions, on educational chats.

Reach Out to Your EduHeroes

In Katherine's first year as an edtech consultant at a local county office, the organization hosted an inaugural edtech event called Tech Rodeo. At the time, many edtech leaders in the area were reading George Couros's book, *Innovator's Mindset: Empower Learning, Unleash Talent, and Lead a Culture of Creativity*. Also, Katherine was impressed by a TED Talk she found online that George had delivered. It was decided. She wanted George Couros to come to Tech Rodeo to deliver a keynote speech.

George Couros had long one been one of Katherine's EduHeroes, and she knew how often he spoke of the power of connections and of social media. Unsure of how to contact him, Katherine started with Twitter. When viewing George's Twitter profile, Katherine was astounded to discover that not only did she follow George—he followed her too! Katherine direct messaged Couros, indicated that the edtech leaders in her area were inspired by his message and asked about his availability for the date of Tech Rodeo. Within twenty minutes, George Couros responded. This example speaks to the nature of the edtech community.

Experts in the field share their knowledge. Since that initial direct message, Katherine has continued to be inspired and encouraged by George. He challenges her to blog weekly, provides her with feedback, and is invaluable in providing perspective regarding professional goals. If Katherine had not had the courage to contact an EduHero, this mentorship may never have occurred. Do not be afraid to reach out to those who inspire you, those you learn from. You never know how a virtual connection may grow organically into something more impactful than you ever anticipated.

> ## DO NOT BE AFRAID TO REACH OUT TO THOSE WHO INSPIRE YOU, THOSE YOU LEARN FROM.

ADAM

I quickly learned how giving the edtech community is, always willing to share ideas, resources, and strategies for free. Even at the beginning of my edtech coaching journey, my tweets, DMs, and e-mails received cordial and relatively prompt responses. Perhaps I was not alone after all. Through Twitter I learned the awesomeness of BookSnaps by following Tara Martin. After tweeting and DM'ing her a few questions, Tara agreed to join me on a video call. For about an hour, I picked her brain about BookSnaps and the research behind it. Tara answered all of my questions and made me feel like a colleague.

Another example of the personable and giving nature of "edtech experts" occurred when I was on a family vacation to Disneyland. While on the Pirates of the Caribbean ride with my youngest daughter, I jokingly tweeted "Currently on Pirates of Caribbean in Disneyland and thinking about teaching. Thx @burgessdave." Within minutes, Dave Burgess responded. He didn't have to respond to an "edtech nobody" like me, but, in the nature of edtech, he empowered me. His simple response made me feel not so lonely. It inspired me to read more of his company's books and to connect with more "edtech experts." At the time, I would not have dreamed that I too would be joining the Dave Burgess Publishing Company as an author. When you continually reach out to a PLN, you may be surprised at the opportunities that come your way in the years to come.

Matt Miller is another titan of the edtech industry who made me feel not so lonely. Following Jon Corippo's advice about Twitter, I participated in many Twitter chats. One of my regular chats was Matt Miller's #DitchBook chat (Thursdays at 7:00 p.m. Pacific). Often on the chat, Matt would ask questions about innovative ideas and feature participant ideas in Top Twenty lists on the Ditch That Textbook blog.

In August of 2015, Matt featured one of Adam's ideas on one of his Top Twenty lists. This was a huge shot in the arm for Adam as a fledgling edtech coach. Your PLN can make you feel noticed, validated, and not so lonely.

The PLN: Connect beyond Your District and IRL

In Katherine's first year out of the classroom, she reached out to coaches and administrators in her district for support and collaboration. These connections were invaluable and she learned a great deal regarding building relationships and approaching teachers with grace and humility. But as a coach who was passionate about edtech and wanted to continue learning effective methods of empowering students via technology integration, Katherine was also hungry for additional learning. She'd never thought of looking past her district for professional learning. Her districts had always had a solid commitment to professional learning opportunities, bringing in curriculum and leadership experts to build educators' capacity. But Katherine had a more specific learning goal.

Her first attempt at learning about edtech was online. Katherine began searching the internet and stumbled upon blog posts, articles, and the occasional website of resources. This information felt static in an industry that was evolving so quickly. This learning felt behind the technology.

Everything changed when Katherine began a Twitter account. After an online search for "edtech Twitter hashtags," she began entering the results into the Twitter search bar. This is where Katherine learned that Google for Education, which was used in her district, had certifications for educators. She also learned that there was such a thing as educational technology conferences, designed specifically to build educator capacity to effectively integrate learning-led technology in education. And Twitter is where she first met Adam, little knowing that a few years later, they would be publishing a book about their professional experiences.

The fight against the loneliness of edtech coaching is not always conducted online and/or with experts. When coaches attend edtech summits, edcamps, and conferences, they connect with their people IRL and have opportunities to learn from and share with those who share their passion for edtech.

ADAM

At these events I mastered the skill of staring at name tags to see if I recognize Twitter handles. This strategy allowed me to first connect with my very good friend, Jeremiah Ruesch. Jeremiah, an expert in his own right, is a math teacher and coach near where I live and work. He and I often were on the same Twitter chats and at the 2016 National CUE Conference, we saw each other's name tags and exclaimed "Hey, I know you from Twitter!" Connecting, in real life, with your online PLN, is a great experience. These serendipitous moments help break down the walls of edtech coach loneliness. The relationships grow organically, nurtured by common professional and personal interests, fed by the desire to continue to develop as educators.

The longer we serve as edtech coaches, helping teachers to integrate technology as they design learning experiences, the more we realize the vast wealth of knowledge in the edtech field. Crowdsourcing questions is powerful. Katherine had discovered #TOSAChat on Twitter, a weekly educational chat for teachers on special assignment. After participating in the chats on a regular basis, she attended an educational conference called Lead 3.0. Here she first learned the power of virtual networks to spark IRL connections.

KATHERINE

I met people with whom I had interacted virtually via #TOSAChat on Twitter. At this conference, I connected with Susan Stewart, an edtech coach from my geographical region. Susan has become a colleague and friend. Our kids play together. She added me to the #TOSAChat Voxer group, which I relied on for professional learning and support nearly every day as I began my edtech coaching journey.

Voxer is a walkie-talkie type app that records all audio and text messages for a group. Like Twitter, it is a great crowdsourcing tool. Many edtech coaches do not have a colleague with a similar role in their building or district. The #TOSAChat Voxer group became my support group, and I was happy to give back to the group when a group member's question matched my experience. When I began my role as an edtech consultant in a county with over forty districts and over two hundred schools, I relied on the Voxer group for support regarding logistics, time management tips, and navigating platforms with which I was previously unfamiliar.

AS AN EDTECH COACH, BE SURE TO FIND A GROUP WITH WHOM TO CROWDSOURCE YOUR QUESTIONS.

A PLN can be built via Twitter, Voxer, Instagram, Facebook, or another collaborative social platform. There is power in numbers. Regardless of the platform selected, get connected. It is through these networks that we can gain ideas, receive feedback, and build relationships to both inspire and encourage us. Edtech coaching will not always be simple. You will not always have the answers. But another edtech coach may have gone through a similar situation. Their support is invaluable.

As you grow your global PLN, it may positively affect your image with colleagues in your district and/or your school site. Katherine's administrators and others have noted, "Everywhere we go someone knows you—they follow you on social media." This statement opens the conversation to share the power of a PLN with those with whom we work on a daily basis. And this can prepare the way for you to begin facilitating PLN building for others.

FACILITATE PLN BUILDING FOR OTHERS

"Katherine and Adam have connected me with other passionate educators through #CVTechTalk. I can go to this PLN when I have any technology questions that will help my students share their learning."

—Monica Figueroa, Teacher, Castle Rock Elementary School, Woodlake Unified School District

As mentioned earlier, edtech coaching can be a lonely job. This can be compounded when working in rural Central California. Each town feels like it is on its own little island. Through our PLN, we discovered amazing edtech and educator learning experiences that were occurring in schools and districts across the region. The problem was that too few educators knew of the great things happening in the town, school, or district just a few miles away.

Consequently, we decided to create #CVTechTalk (the CV stands for Central Valley of California), a Twitter hashtag and edchat, as a platform to help build bridges between these towns, schools, and districts. It was designed to be a space for educators to share all the great strategies they were implementing in their classrooms. #CVTechTalk is a place to build up fellow educators, promote ideas, get feedback, and give teacher/student work an authentic audience.

#CVTechTalk began as a weekly Twitter chat, and is still going strong, on Wednesdays at 7:00 p.m. Pacific. Soon, we realized that to reach more educators, we needed to expand to other platforms. In recent years, Facebook Groups have taken off. We started a #CVTechTalk group on Facebook and soon saw that there are many educators who are not on Twitter, but are on the Facebook platform. From there we created a community on the now defunct Google+ platform, as well as a group on Voxer. We created a sticker with the hashtag and time of the chat, which we hand out every chance we get. We promote the chat on our vehicles on license plate frames in addition to writing #CVTechTalk updates with window chalk on the windows of our offices.

And like our individual edtech vehicles, this all grew organically. It began as a seed idea, to leverage Twitter to facilitate connections among California's Central Valley, but has since grown beyond our region and onto other platforms. #CVTechTalk is not about us, it is about serving others.

 IN ORDER FOR AN IDEA TO GROW, YOU MUST OBSERVE THE NEEDS OF YOUR ENVIRONMENT.

It is through our conversations with others, through our observations of social media platforms, that #CVTechTalk developed into what it is today. It was developed as a response to educators in our area looking to connect and learn.

Soon we began broadcasting a simulcast of the Twitter chat on Facebook Live, where we read the tweets and added some banter and commentary. Network members enjoy watching and commenting along, particularly because—while on professional topics—these interactions let our personalities shine through on video. Those we serve want to see that we are human beings, that we have hobbies and interests, that we interact with others personally as well as professionally.

We were pleasantly surprised to discover our reach grew organically to stretch beyond our region. #CVTechTalk was originally designed to connect educators in the rural Central Valley of California. Now educators from around the world regularly join in. One example is Dr. Kirk Henwood from Colorado. Kirk connected with us and picked our brains for ways to better empower his college students. After a few phone conversations, Kirk now facilitates his own Twitter chat as part of his college courses.

On a semiregular basis, Israeli educator Noa Lahav joins the chat. #CVTechTalk occurs at 5:00 a.m. on Israeli time. Whenever she is up early, Noa makes a point to join in. We had the privilege of meeting Noa in person at the 2019 ISTE conference in Philadelphia, and chatted for over an hour. The opportunity to meet and chat with Noa is concrete proof of the bridges built by #CVTechTalk. After that real-life conversation, Noa continued to reach out to us to help connect her with Google for Education in an attempt to create a Google Educator Group (GEG) in Israel.

Whether you are trying to create your own chat or participate in one, consistency is the key. In over three years of #CVTechTalk, we have only missed one Wednesday. That miss was due to exhaustion after ISTE 2018 in Chicago, when we had simply forgotten to schedule the tweets before heading to the airport. Upon landing, we had dozens of tweets asking what happened to the weekly chat.

WHETHER YOU ARE TRYING TO CREATE YOUR OWN CHAT OR PARTICIPATE IN ONE, CONSISTENCY IS THE KEY.

Consistent participation on Twitter chats and/or other methods of connection to your PLN is crucial. Consistency fosters an organic development into what is akin to an online, educational version of the sitcom *Cheers*. It's where everybody knows your name and they're always glad you came. Being a regular in these groups helps you take control of your professional learning. Your development will grow according to the context of your needs. If we do not know enough about something, our PLN can almost always connect us with someone who does. As a collective, we are a powerful resource.

Tips to get started facilitating and joining a social media chat

Join and Participate	Facilitate
• Connect with participants on social media (follow on Twitter, friend on Facebook, etc.) • Begin conversations—ask participants to elaborate on topics or ideas that spark your interest • Don't be afraid to respond to people's tweets and Facebook posts	• Be consistent (we have found weekly chats are most effective) • Promote on multiple channels (social media, stickers, reminders on your office window, etc.) • Welcome participants and be liberal with your likes, retweets, and responses • Follow participants and encourage them to follow each other to build their PLN

– CHAPTER 19 –

WORK-LIFE FUSION

The need for work-life balance is prevalent in our society. As human beings, it is vital that we attend to our personal lives as well as our professional lives. And yet, the term balance suggests that we have two *separate* lives, one for work and another for life. We prefer to use the term *work-life fusion*. While at work, we are still friends, parents, spouses, and fans of sports and music. At work, we don't stop being passionate fans of Fresno State athletics or jazz music or Manchester United or Disney. Those things are part of us 24-7. Those passions enhance our work.

Away from work, in our life, we remain educators. If we are in a classroom and see a STEM challenge one of our daughters will like, we take note of it to bring back home. When we are home and see a commercial or a movie clip that fits well in a professional learning session we plan to facilitate, we will take note to add it in. At family dinnertime, we never shy away from talking about work. Talking about work often leads to meaningful banter with our children. The fusion between work and life develops organically, naturally. There is no work-life on/off switch.

> # AS INDIVIDUALS, AS OUR PROFESSIONAL AND PERSONAL LIVES MELD TOGETHER, THEY CAN COMPLEMENT AND SUPPORT EACH OTHER RATHER THAN BE IN OPPOSITION.

To achieve a work-life fusion, it is crucial to have a close relationship with someone who respects your professional life—and passion—as an educator. It is very difficult to live between two worlds.

KATHERINE

In a previous relationship, I was criticized for my optimism and passion for education. I was told I cared too much about the students and teachers I served, that I was naive to believe that I could ever make a difference. This negativity and cynicism was toxic. I was continually reminded about balance and told that what I needed was more time completely removed from work. The message was that I needed to shed my identity as an educator when away from campus, to separate myself into distinct work and life categories that did not mix. But what my soul craved was a fusion between the two.

I had to make tough decisions. I began to spend more time with those who lifted me up, who valued me for what makes me who I am—as a parent, friend, individual, and educator. I cut ties with an individual who did not feed my soul. I do not propose that we discard relationships haphazardly. The lack of support for my career was merely one symptom among many, revealing a relationship that was beyond repair. But this is a reminder to remain true to who we are, to continually seek to feed our souls. I chose to create a work-life fusion. As a result, I felt fully authentic. I was able to completely be me in all areas of my life, work and personal. And (though I did not expect this) I experienced unprecedented growth both personally and professionally.

Adam's path toward work-life fusion involved reaching out more.

ADAM

It's no coincidence that the cultivation of tremendous life-giving friendships and experiences happened around the same time as a period of massive growth for me professionally. Since becoming a connected educator, with a large PLN, I have made some of the best, life-giving friendships of my entire life. Both online and in-person, when I see and interact with these friends, my soul is refreshed. Receiving a tweet or Facebook response from these people puts a smile on my face. Seeing them in person at a conference is utter joy.

One of those friends is Martin Cisneros. The second I see Martin, we both start spitting out jokes, catchphrases, and Wu-Tang Clan references. The time we spend together with our "edtech amigos" is an absolute blast. I have learned much from Martin over the years about using edtech to empower English learners. This professional relationship has blossomed into such a great friendship that he was one of my groomsmen when Katherine and I had our wedding at Fall CUE 2018.

Yes, you read that correctly. Katherine and I got hitched at an edtech conference, Fall CUE, onstage, with our PLN member and mentor Jon Corippo officiating in 2018. The ceremony was on the conference schedule for anyone to attend as well as streamed by CUE on Facebook Live. Work-life fusion, for us, means inviting our PLN into our personal lives, and vice versa. This is not to say that all must be public, but it is to say that we are authentically ourselves at all times. To be clear, we are not suggesting that in order to have a work-life fusion, it is necessary to be married to an educator interested in edtech, or that you must get married or renew your vows at an edtech conference. It is a part of our story, one that occurred because of our work-life fusion, but your story will be unique to your context—it will be organic. We believe if you look to have work and life portions of your life complement each other, it allows you to be truly yourself throughout your daily activities.

What might work-life fusion look like for you? You might begin by including images of your family, friends, or hobbies on an intro slide when you facilitate a professional learning session. When those you serve see you as a human being, you become more than just an "edtech coach." You can spark connections that go past technological platforms and apps. Education, above all, is a relationship business. We serve people, not mandates, test scores, or technological platforms. Nothing can replace the power of a personal connection.

Since our public marriage ceremony, a few people have approached us with the remark, "You don't know me, but I was at your wedding!" When we share something about our personal lives with those we serve, we are better able to connect and collaborate on a deeper level. Be authentic, be you, and be real. It matters more than you may realize.

> BE AUTHENTIC, BE YOU, AND BE REAL. IT MATTERS MORE THAN YOU MAY REALIZE.

It is not natural for Katherine to begin a professional conversation on a personal note. Her personality is such that she likes to get to business first and move to the personal afterward. However, she was at an improvement science workshop that discussed a professional conversational technique called rounding. The first step of rounding is to begin with a personal question regarding the colleague with which you are having a conversation. Katherine challenged herself to try this, because beginning with the person rather than the work was an opportunity for growth. Soon, she began to implement the strategy.

Katherine found that when she began conversations by asking about teachers' weekends, travels, or children, they felt more comfortable and this leads to more effective work. This surprised Katherine, but she enjoyed the conversations more as well! And she enjoys building organic relationships with those she serves. And when she opens up about her personal life with those being coached, they are more likely to feel they can relate to her. We are, simply, in a people business.

WE SERVE LEARNERS, NOT INITIATIVES.

Our focus must be on humans. It is who we are and the most important part of our roles.

Our children are a huge part of our work-life fusion. For those who don't know, we have four children between the two of us. Dillon, Katherine's son, is seventeen. Adam has three daughters, Ashleigh (eight), Arielle (seven) and Andrina (six). They have grown up with edtech.

When Adam's daughters were younger, he participated in Twitter edchats while bathing them. Now, the weekly #CVTechTalk edchat that he and Katherine founded is a part of his daughters' lives and weekly routine too. They know when it is #CVTechTalk time. They know that Katherine and I will be on our computers tweeting and talking about tweets on Facebook Live. Quite often, they will join for a couple of minutes, on camera, saying hello and answering questions that relate to the chat.

It has been quite insightful to have students provide perspective during these educational chats. This builds pride in our children about the work we do, and also engages them in the work with us. Ashleigh and Arielle will sometimes be nearby during the #CVTechTalks, playing games on their Chromebooks. They have even told their teachers to check out #CVTechTalk. All of our children have attended the Tech Rodeo edtech conference we helped organize, and two of them actually led a session at the conference about #BookSnaps, the close-reading strategy that mixes Snapchat and text.

We are not only educators at home. And we aren't the only ones with a similar work-life fusion. At many of the same conferences, events, and edchats, you will see our friend Rebekah Remkievicz and her children copresenting sessions. Our friend Ben Cogswell also brings his children to help with his sessions. We are working with Ben on planning an edtech family camping trip in the near future.

When we encounter members of our PLN, usually the first thing people ask about is how the kids are doing. They've watched our kids grow up, through the power of Facebook. Whenever Adam runs into his treasured PLN friend Josh Harris, Josh always asks about the kids and only calls them by their nicknames. Three years ago, when Adam's daughter Andrina had open-heart surgery, Adam posted hour-by-hour updates of her surgery and recovery on social media. The majority of the responses, prayers, and well wishes were from people in our PLN, including Josh.

It's natural for this work-life fusion to evolve to the point where the lines are blurred between PLN colleagues and friends. Many people are simply both. Judy Blakeney and Adam were cohort mates at the Sydney 2017 Google Innovator Academy, giving each other tons of valuable feedback while there. Since then, they use each other as sounding boards for ideas and strategies. And when driving through Judy's neck of the woods in Mission Viejo, California, Katherine and Adam are treated to amazing hospitality in the form of her husband's amazing cooking.

Friends from outside our PLN and the world of education also greatly support what we do. This past fall, at Adam's twenty-year high school reunion, a former classmate, Joey, who Adam hadn't seen since graduation applauded the work we do and shared on Facebook. He watches us on Facebook Live every week. Joey, a farmer, has an idea about connecting with STEM teachers about lessons with drones. His farm does a lot of work with drones and he was interested in what students today are learning about them.

Work-life fusion serves to nourish our souls, but it can do even more than that. The more authentic we become as edtech coaches, the more effective are our relationships with those we serve. Authenticity is underrated. Our community of educators, family, and friends respect someone who is real, who is human, and who cares enough to ask them about their own lives.

TIPS FOR WORK-LIFE FUSION

Commuting to and from work is a necessary part of the daily routine. In the car, we are 100 percent educators and 100 percent human. During this daily commute, artificial intelligence can support efficiency. Google Assistant can be been an invaluable tool for maintaining a work-life fusion. It allows you to keep your eyes on the road while answering and voice-composing texts with friends, family, and colleagues. Later in the day, it's possible to coordinate dinner and child pickup via Google Assistant voice texting. This feature is also available for Siri and other platforms.

As an organic edtech coach, being available to those you serve is essential. However, sometimes being *too* available can lead to overload. We are only human. Here the snooze function in Gmail can be invaluable in maintaining sanity when a deluge of e-mails come through. This tool allows us to postpone our response without losing the reminder.

Katherine is usually at school sites working with educators. Sometimes the e-mail notifications on her phone could prevent her from truly being present with the educators she serves. But she doesn't want to miss dinner with her family because she's spending time catching up on e-mails. So, to minimize stress and maximize impact, Katherine began answering e-mails each morning at home, while drinking her coffee. This fuses work and life together and allows her to receive an e-mail notification during the day with the confidence that there is time allotted for a response.

Work-life fusion is not simple. Your methods of an effective fusion will be unique to you.

"I think my favorite thing about using social media to connect with others is that I can ask a question at pretty much any time of day and someone will respond with suggestions. Random ideas and questions pop into my head constantly, and social media gives me a place to ask and flesh out ideas with people that I may not have access to IRL [in real life].

Almost every Wed night at 7:00 I do #CVTechTalk during bath time. We're usually done about fifteen minutes into the chat. I used to participate in some chats while waiting for my son at speech therapy and my other son at swim lessons."

—Kim Calderon, high school teacher, Madera Unified

This fusion of work and life gives you authenticity. Your life is not only in balance; each facet is complementary to each other. And just like edtech coaching, there is no one-size-fits-all approach to work-life fusion. But authenticity is key.

HIGHLIGHT REEL: PART IV

TAKEAWAYS

Edtech coaches have to keep learning in order to keep teaching.

- Educational technology iterates quickly: certifications and badges keep you growing and increase your clout.
- PLNs are essential to combat loneliness and increase impact.
- Facilitating PLNs for others increases your own knowledge.
- Work-life fusion increases meaning for you and learning for those you serve.

QUESTIONS FOR REFLECTION

- How do you feed yourself regarding professional learning? What steps will you take to move forward (i.e., certifications, participation in social media groups)?
- What have been your methods of becoming a connected educator? How might you continue to grow your PLN?
- Are the educators you serve connected to a PLN? How might you encourage them to be involved, or facilitate a platform to connect them with other educators?

BRAINSTORMING GUIDE

What professional certifications or badges would give you pride?

What steps can you take today to move toward achieving these certifications?

What might have held you back from achieving these certifications? How might you overcome these obstacles?

Have you ever felt the lack of a personal support network? How did you overcome it?

What would work-life fusion mean for you? What could block you from achieving that integration?

THE SEND-OFF

Organic edtech coaching is not about us. It is centered on cultivating environments that spark educational growth. As you observe your own environment, as you build relationships with educators and students in your midst, remember to be authentic. As an edtech coach, you matter. Your work is enormously valuable and can make a difference in inspiring educators and students alike to innovate with an inquisitive spirit.

 AS AN EDTECH COACH, YOU MATTER.

Never forget that as an edtech coach, you are much more than a PD delivery system. You are an educator first: tools are secondary. As you continue in the good work you are doing for the sake of students, remember to feed yourself before facilitating growth in others. Thank you for all you do. It is edtech coaches like yourself, those who are striving for personal growth and seeking to improve the conditions of their environment, who are truly a blessing to today's students.

RESOURCES

Books

- Jimmy Casas, *What Connected Educators Do Differently*
- George Couros, *The Innovator's Mindset: Empower Learning, Unleash Talent, and Lead a Culture of Creativity*
- Marlena Hebern, Jon Corippo, *The EduProtocol Field Guide Book 2: 12 New Lesson Frames for Even More Engagement*
- Matt Miller, *Ditch That Textbook*
- Daniel Pink, *Drive: The Surprising Truth about What Motivates Us*

Website Links

- Crunchbase statistics: www.edscoop.com
- BookSnaps: www.tarammartin.com
- How to make appointment slots in Google Calendar: bit.ly/GCAppointmentSlots
- FormMule: bit.ly/FormMuleExtension
- Cardinal Innovation Center: cardinalinnovationcenter.org

PLN Educators Mentioned

- Janell Miller: @IamJanellM
- Joe Marquez: @JoeMarquez70
- Sean Fahey: @seanjfahey
- Karly Moura: @karlymoura
- Evan Mosier: @emosier3

- George Couros: @gcouros
- John Eick: @john_eick
- Tara Martin: @taramartinedu
- Matt Miller: @jmattmiller
- Susan Stewart: @techcoachsusan
- Kyla Henwood: @khenwood
- Noa Lahav: @supervxn
- Martin Cisneros: @thetechprofe
- Jon Corippo: @jcorippo
- Judy Blakeney: @judyblakeney

ABOUT THE AUTHORS

KATHERINE GOYETTE

Katherine Goyette has been in education for over fifteen years. She has been a classroom teacher in grades K, 1, 2, 5, and 6; a county office consultant; an academic coach; administrator; and instructor of preservice and intern teachers. Prior to her work in the public education sector, Katherine taught music classes for students of all ages, from infants through adults. She is a Google Certified Educator, Trainer, Innovator. Katherine was primary writer for California's Computer Science Standards and is a region lead for the California Digital Learning / Computer Science Collaborative. Learn more about Katherine at wonderexplorelearn.com or on Twitter at @kat_goyette.

ADAM JUAREZ

Adam Juarez has taught US and world history and served as 6–12 technology integration coach at the middle and high school levels in Orosi, CA, for fifteen years. Additionally, Adam serves as an instructor for preservice teachers and interns in Tulare County. He is a Google Certified Educator, Trainer, and Innovator and frequently speaks and presents at CUE, ISTE, KCI, and edtech conferences. Learn more about Adam at techcoachjuarez.com and connect with him on Twitter or Instagram at @techcoachjuarez.

SPEAKING

Bring AdaKat to You

Adam and Katherine are available for both keynotes and workshops on a variety of topics. Select from a topic below or contact them to customize a message to meet your needs.

AdaKat:

- Distance Learning for ALL
- 4Cs Lesson Design: Lead with Learning, Never with Tech
- Work-Life Fusion
- Coaching Trumps PD
- The Walking Coach
- Connect with Tech-Hesitant Teachers
- Organic EdTech with G#Suite (Google for Education)

Adam:

- Ditch That Copier
- The Versatile World of Sketchnoting
    - Reimagine Images
    - Slide into BookSnaps
    - Set Your Sites on Galleries
- Google Certification (educator and student editions available)
- Google Classroom: Launchpad for Learning
- Phone Friendly Lesson Design

Katherine:

- Support Students with SEL Utilizing EdTech
- EdTech for Young Learners
- Universal Design for Learning for Professional Learning
- Access for ALL: UDL in the Classroom
- Leverage EdTech for English Learners and Students with Special Needs
- Beyond an Hour of Code: Computer Science for K–8
- STEAM/PBL: Relevant & Engaging!
- Future Ready Leadership

Contact Adam and Katherine via e-mail at adakatedtechconsulting@gmail.com

MORE FROM

DAVE BURGESS Consulting, Inc.

Since 2012, DBCI has been publishing books that inspire and equip educators to be their best. For more information on our titles or to purchase bulk orders for your school, district, or book study, visit DaveBurgessconsulting.com/DBCIbooks.

More Technology & Tools

50 Things You Can Do with Google Classroom by Alice Keeler and Libbi Miller

50 Things to Go Further with Google Classroom by Alice Keeler and Libbi Miller

140 Twitter Tips for Educators by Brad Currie, Billy Krakower, and Scott Rocco

Block Breaker by Brian Aspinall

Code Breaker by Brian Aspinall

Control Alt Achieve by Eric Curts

Google Apps for Littles by Christine Pinto and Alice Keeler

Master the Media by Julie Smith

Reality Bytes by Christine Lion-Bailey, Jesse Lubinsky, and Micah Shippee, PhD

Sail the 7 Cs with Microsoft Education by Becky Keene and Kathi Kersznowski

Shake Up Learning by Kasey Bell

Social LEADia by Jennifer Casa-Todd

Stepping Up to Google Classroom by Alice Keeler and
Kimberly Mattina

Teaching Math with Google Apps by Alice Keeler and
Diana Herrington

Teachingland by Amanda Fox and Mary Ellen Weeks

Like a PIRATE™ Series

Teach Like a PIRATE by Dave Burgess

eXPlore Like a Pirate by Michael Matera

Learn Like a Pirate by Paul Solarz

Play Like a Pirate by Quinn Rollins

Run Like a Pirate by Adam Welcome

Tech Like a PIRATE by Matt Miller

Lead Like a PIRATE™ Series

Lead Like a PIRATE by Shelley Burgess and Beth Houf

Balance Like a Pirate by Jessica Cabeen, Jessica Johnson, and
Sarah Johnson

Lead beyond Your Title by Nili Bartley

Lead with Appreciation by Amber Teamann and Melinda Miller

Lead with Culture by Jay Billy

Lead with Instructional Rounds by Vicki Wilson

Lead with Literacy by Mandy Ellis

Leadership & School Culture

Culturize by Jimmy Casas

Escaping the School Leader's Dunk Tank by Rebecca Coda and
Rick Jetter

Fight Song by Kim Bearden

From Teacher to Leader by Starr Sackstein

If the Dance Floor Is Empty, Change the Song by Joe Clark

The Innovator's Mindset by George Couros

It's OK to Say "They" by Christy Whittlesey

Kids Deserve It! by Todd Nesloney and Adam Welcome

Let Them Speak by Rebecca Coda and Rick Jetter

The Limitless School by Abe Hege and Adam Dovico

Live Your Excellence by Jimmy Casas

Next-Level Teaching by Jonathan Alsheimer

The Pepper Effect by Sean Gaillard

The Principled Principal by Jeffrey Zoul and Anthony McConnell

Relentless by Hamish Brewer

The Secret Solution by Todd Whitaker, Sam Miller, and Ryan Donlan

Start. Right. Now. by Todd Whitaker, Jeffrey Zoul, and Jimmy Casas

Stop. Right. Now. by Jimmy Casas and Jeffrey Zoul

Teachers Deserve It by Rae Hughart and Adam Welcome

Teach Your Class Off by CJ Reynolds

They Call Me "Mr. De" by Frank DeAngelis

Thrive through the Five by Jill M. Siler

Unmapped Potential by Julie Hasson and Missy Lennard

When Kids Lead by Todd Nesloney and Adam Dovico

Word Shift by Joy Kirr

Your School Rocks by Ryan McLane and Eric Lowe

Teaching Methods & Materials

All 4s and 5s by Andrew Sharos

Boredom Busters by Katie Powell

The Classroom Chef by John Stevens and Matt Vaudrey

The Collaborative Classroom by Trevor Muir

Copyrighteous by Diana Gill

CREATE by Bethany J. Petty

Ditch That Homework by Matt Miller and Alice Keeler

Ditch That Textbook by Matt Miller

Don't Ditch That Tech by Matt Miller, Nate Ridgway, and Angelia Ridgway

EDrenaline Rush by John Meehan

Educated by Design by Michael Cohen, The Tech Rabbi

The EduProtocol Field Guide by Marlena Hebern and Jon Corippo
The EduProtocol Field Guide: Book 2 by Marlena Hebern and
    Jon Corippo
Instant Relevance by Denis Sheeran
LAUNCH by John Spencer and A.J. Juliani
Make Learning MAGICAL by Tisha Richmond
Pure Genius by Don Wettrick
The Revolution by Darren Ellwein and Derek McCoy
Shift This! by Joy Kirr
Skyrocket Your Teacher Coaching by Michael Cary Sonbert
Spark Learning by Ramsey Musallam
Sparks in the Dark by Travis Crowder and Todd Nesloney
Table Talk Math by John Stevens
The Wild Card by Hope and Wade King
The Writing on the Classroom Wall by Steve Wyborney

Inspiration, Professional Growth & Personal Development

Be REAL by Tara Martin
Be the One for Kids by Ryan Sheehy
The Coach ADVenture by Amy Illingworth
Creatively Productive by Lisa Johnson
Educational Eye Exam by Alicia Ray
The EduNinja Mindset by Jennifer Burdis
Empower Our Girls by Lynmara Colón and Adam Welcome
Finding Lifelines by Andrew Grieve and Andrew Sharos
The Four O'Clock Faculty by Rich Czyz
How Much Water Do We Have? by Pete and Kris Nunweiler
P Is for Pirate by Dave and Shelley Burgess
A Passion for Kindness by Tamara Letter
The Path to Serendipity by Allyson Apsey
Sanctuaries by Dan Tricarico
The SECRET SAUCE by Rich Czyz
Shattering the Perfect Teacher Myth by Aaron Hogan

Stories from Webb by Todd Nesloney

Talk to Me by Kim Bearden

Teach Better by Chad Ostrowski, Tiffany Ott, Rae Hughart, and Jeff Gargas

Teach Me, Teacher by Jacob Chastain

Teach, Play, Learn! by Adam Peterson

The Teachers of Oz by Herbie Raad and Nathan Lang-Raad

TeamMakers by Laura Robb and Evan Robb

Through the Lens of Serendipity by Allyson Apsey

The Zen Teacher by Dan Tricarico

Children's Books

Beyond Us by Aaron Polansky

Cannonball In by Tara Martin

Dolphins in Trees by Aaron Polansky

I Want to Be a Lot by Ashley Savage

The Princes of Serendip by Allyson Apsey

The Wild Card Kids by Hope and Wade King

Zom-Be a Design Thinker by Amanda Fox

Made in the USA
Las Vegas, NV
12 July 2021